Our

# of Lo

Paul De Marco

ISBN : 9798746651952

Words of Bernadette

"I want my whole life to be inspired by love."

"When I see her I feel as if I'm no longer of this world. And when the vision disappears I'm amazed to find myself still here."

"Yes, dear Mother, you have come down to the earth to appear to a weak child. You, Queen of heaven and earth, have chosen what was the most humble according to the world."

"I was nothing, and of this nothing God made something great. In Holy Communion I am heart to heart with Jesus. How sublime is my destiny."

"The grotto was my Heaven; You will find me there at the foot of the rock."

"I noticed that Our Blessed Lady would often look over my head to single out individuals in the crowd. She would then smile on them as though they were old familiar friends."

"This would be the last time I would see her on this earth. I knew, because my Lady had prepared my soul for Jesus, and she would give me now to Him with whom I had communed. I knew, because of the way she held her head as she said goodbye. She left heaven in my heart and it has been there ever since."

"I have seen her. How beautiful she is, and how I long to go to her."

"Life is only heaven's waiting room!"

- Contents -

Introduction

Chapter 1: **A saint born into chaos**   (page 8)

Chapter 2: **Apparitions of Our Lady**   (page 16)

Chapter 3: **A life changed forever**   (page 48)

Chapter 4: **The long road to sainthood**   (page 69)

Chapter 5: **God's plan for Mankind**   (page 79)

Chapter 6: **Mary, The Immaculate Conception**   (page 94)

Chapter 7: **A call to repentance**   (page 103)

Chapter 8: **The Lourdes - Fatima link**   (page 118)

Chapter 9: **The Rosary**   (page 133)

- Introduction -

Bernadette Soubirous, a 14 year old girl from Lourdes in the Pyrenees, claimed to have seen an apparition of a beautiful lady at a grotto in a cliff outside the town on 11th February 1858.

Despite the hostility and disbelief of those who thought that she was delusional, Bernadette continued to visit the grotto at Massabielle, and over a period of five months there were a total of 18 apparitions.

At the 9th apparition on 25th February, a crowd of a few hundred people watched her scratch at the ground, and a small pool of water began to form there, which soon turned into a spring.

Bernadette said that the lady had asked her to dig at that very spot with her bare hands, and within days there were reports of miraculous healings involving people who had drunk or touched the water there.

However, she was still treated with derision by many, especially those in authority, but on 25th March Bernadette told a priest named Father Peyramale that the Lady had said, **"I am the Immaculate Conception."**

This shattering revelation convinced him that the apparitions were indeed genuine as there was no way that the uneducated Bernadette could possibly have understood the meaning of this title.

Unsurprisingly, these events changed Bernadette's life forever and she joined the Sisters of Charity of Nevers where she cared for the sick in the hospice.

An Episcopal Commission was set up by Bishop Laurence of Tarbes to rigorously investigate Bernadette's life and to take eye witness statements of people who'd been present at the apparitions.

A team of doctors investigated all the reported claims of miraculous cures, discussing their cases with the doctors who'd been treating them over the years and then re-examining the patients themselves.

After three and a half years, Bishop Laurence announced the conclusion of the Commission on 18th January 1862, stating that the faithful were justified in believing the events at Lourdes with certainty.

Doctor Vergez was one of the leading doctors on the medical panel which reviewed all the cases of spontaneous healings at Lourdes. He concluded his lengthy investigation by saying: 'Such phenomena are beyond the comprehension of the human mind."

Regarding those people who'd disbelieved and derided her for so long, Bernadette said, "All finally believed in the Apparitions, and died with the crucifix pressed to their lips."

Bernadette lived in poverty and at a time when infant mortality was about 158 per 1000 live births and where the average life expectancy of a woman was just 41 years, and even lower for men. Four of Bernadette's siblings died as infants and another died at the age of nine.

The country was afflicted by diseases like dysentery and typhoid fever, and there were cholera pandemics which claimed hundreds of thousands of lives in France. Bernadette herself contracted cholera as a child and was sickly as a result of the infection for the rest of her life.

The wheat and potato crops of the country were often blighted as well, causing widespread famine and civil unrest. So Bernadette's life was never far from suffering and she passed away at the age of just 35 on 16th April 1879.

Her remains were exhumed three times and on the last of these exhumations, which was conducted by Doctor Comte 46 years after her death, Bernadette's body was still found to be incorrupt and undecayed. The doctor was absolutely stunned to see that her liver appeared to be 'almost normal' prompting him to report that this was not a natural phenomenon.

Since 1858 there have been thousands of reported miraculous cures of which 70 have been accepted by the Church after the most stringent investigation, and several of these are discussed in the book. But the legacy of Lourdes is that it's become a site of pilgrimage which has drawn an estimated 200 million people there since 1858.

The 18 apparitions at Lourdes and the 6 at Fatima 59 years later shouldn't be viewed in isolation, because there's a synergy between them and they complement each other very well.

In both cases there was a call to repentance and the conversion of sinners, and at Lourdes and Fatima Our Lady worked spectacular miracles to prove that the apparitions were genuine. The most incredible of these was the Miracle of the Sun on 13th October 1917 which was witnessed by a crowd of about 70,000.

At Lourdes Our Lady announced that she was The Immaculate Conception, and at two of the apparitions at Fatima she referred to 'Her Immaculate Heart.'

So as the two sets of apparitions have so much in common, one of the chapters of the book looks into what we can learn from the shared message of Lourdes and Fatima.

At the apparitions in Lourdes, Our Lady prayed the Rosary with Bernadette, and at all 6 apparitions in Fatima Our Lady asked the children to pray the Rosary each day. Now as this formed such an intrinsic part of Our Lady's message, there's a chapter that looks at the 20 mysteries of the Rosary, which will help anyone who likes to make this devotion.

But are the events at Lourdes and the message that Our Lady gave to Bernadette in 1858 relevant to us now?

Quite simply, the message of Lourdes doesn't belong in our history books but in our hearts, and the message of Our Lady couldn't be more important for us than it is today.

Mary appeared in Lourdes at a time of poverty, famine and disease, to give us hope and to draw us to the love of God, and she did the same again at Fatima in 1917. The book examines what Our Lady said, and reveals why she, The Immaculate Conception, is a unique and essential part in God's plan for mankind.

Mary knows her son Jesus better than anyone who has ever lived, and if we allow her to, she will draw us closer to his love and walk with us along the road which leads to eternal life.

- Chapter 1 -

A Saint born into chaos

Bernadette Soubirous was born on 7th January 1844, in the small garrison town of Lourdes which had a population of around four thousand and which nestled in the foothills of the magnificent Pyrenees.

At this time, Jean-de-Dieu Soult was the Prime Minister of France, Nicholas I was the Emperor of Russia, Sir Robert Peel was Prime Minister of Great Britain, and John Tyler was the 10th President of the United States.

Bernadette was born on the first floor of an old flour mill, named the Boly Mill, which was operated by her father Francois at the time. Three years before Bernadette was born, Augustin Casterot, who was the miller of the Boly Mill at the time, was killed in a road accident on 1st July 1841. This tragedy suddenly left his widow Claire with absolutely no means to support herself and her six children.

It was then that Claire asked Francois, who'd been working at another flour mill nearby, to help her run the Boly Mill. Francois was 34 years of age and still a bachelor when he started working there, but his single days soon came to an end when he fell in love with Louise, who was one of Claire Casterot's daughters. They were married on 9th January 1843, when Francois was 35 and Louise was just 17 years of age, and they soon set up home together in the mill, living together with Claire and all her children.

In time, Louise and Francois came to be known as the 'Millers of Boly' and they were well-liked in the town because of their kindness and hospitality. Francois was an honest, hard working man, and when his clients brought their wheat to be ground in the mill, Louise invariably prepared them a full meal to eat while they were waiting.

They were also generous to any beggars who passed by and Francois sometimes ground wheat for his poor clients without charging them anything for it. This generosity put a strain on their finances, because, amongst all the other costs, they had to find 250 francs a year just to cover their rent.

Bernadette was born almost exactly a year after their marriage and she was baptised two days later on 9ᵗʰ January 1844, in an old granite font in St Pierre's, which was their local parish church. (The font is still used today for baptisms.) This special day was also the date of their first wedding anniversary. Her baptismal name was actually Marie-Bernard, but from her early childhood days everyone simply called her Bernadette.

By now, France had entered the industrial revolution, which meant that many workers in labour-intensive industries such as the textiles industry, mining and farming, had lost their jobs due to the advent of mechanisation.

However, the banks hadn't evolved to keep pace with the credit needs of the growing French economy, and the country also lacked a decent railway infrastructure to transport raw materials around the country. Despite the move to industrialisation, by far the largest sector of the French economy was still agriculture at this time. The great French revolutions of 1789 and 1830 had both been fueled by poor grain harvests, and once again a shortage of grain would soon spark yet another revolution in the country.

At the mill, Louise suffered a severe burn in November 1844 when the molten wax of a tallow (animal fat) candle set her breast on fire. Bernadette was only 10 months old at the time, and to make matters worse, Louise was already pregnant with her second child by then. The injury meant that she could no longer breast feed Bernadette and so she put her into the care of a wet nurse named Marie Aravant Lagues, who lived at Burg House in the village of Bartres, which was about 6 kilometres from Lourdes.

Infant mortality was very high at this time and Marie had tragically lost her own son when he was just 18 days old. Francois and Louise paid Marie 5 francs a month to care for their young baby girl and Francois went to visit Bernadette in Bartres whenever he could find the time to do so.

Louise later gave birth to a baby boy on 13ᵗʰ February 1845 and they named him Jean, but sadly he passed away when he was only two months old.

Understandably Marie grew very fond of the baby that she'd breast fed until October 1845, but she returned Bernadette to her mother at the Boly Mill when she was 21 months old. Her return would have been a great comfort to Louise who'd only just turned 20 years of age.

Marie later said this of Bernadette: "As a baby, Bernadette was already very loveable, the neighbours loved to see her and to hold her in their arms. You could not stop loving her enough, she was sweet and loveable."

Mills like the Boly Mill were now coming under pressure from the more efficient steam mills that were springing up all around the country, and to exacerbate the situation, there were poor cereal harvests in both 1845 and 1846. The low wheat yield unfortunately coincided with a severe blight of the potato crop in those same years.

1845 also marked the beginning of a seven year period in Ireland known as the Great Famine, which killed at least a million people, with higher estimates being 1.5 million, and which resulted in a similar number emigrating from the country.

But despite the worsening economic outlook for the Soubirous family, Louise fell pregnant again and gave birth to Marie Antoinette on 19th September 1846. She was affectionately called 'Toinette' and was two and a half years younger than Bernadette.

By June 1847, the price of wheat was two and a half times higher than it had been in 1844. This pushed the cost of a loaf of bread to 52 centimes at a time when the average pay for a labourer was just two francs a day. Bread was the staple food of the workers, and so the increased price soon had a negative impact on the profits of labour-intensive industries such as textiles and construction, and this quickly led to mass unemployment. Angry crowds, tired of the worsening economic situation, flooded the streets of Paris on 22nd February 1848, leading to the collapse of the French Government and forcing King Louise Philippe to flee to the safety of England.

The disastrous grain harvests also put a huge strain on small, inefficient mills like the Boly Mill that Francois was operating. Claire Casterot (Louise's mother) left the Boly Mill with her own children in 1848 and moved into the home where her eldest daughter was living with her husband. This relieved a great deal of pressure on the overcrowded conditions in the mill, but with Claire's departure, a wealth of experience in how to run a flour mill went walking out the door as well. It was in late 1848 that Francois was injured in an accident while repairing his millstone, when a stone chip flew into his face, and he was left blinded for life in his left eye as a result.

Louise gave birth to a baby boy on 18th December 1848, who they named Jean Marie. At the time, Bernadette was a few weeks short of her 5th birthday, and she already had her hands full helping her poor mother look after her siblings. These would have been harsh times indeed for the residents of Lourdes, because many of them were labourers on the farms and in the quarries. The Soubirous family struggled on, but they were soon faced with another tragedy with the death of Jean-Marie at just two years of age, on 4th January 1851. Louise was pregnant at the time of his death, and when she gave birth to another baby boy on 13th May 1851, they named him Jean Marie.

On 5th October 1853, the Crimean War began between the Ottoman Turks and Russia. Britain and France entered the war in January 1854, coming to the assistance of Turkey in order to prevent further Russian territorial gains. It was a catastrophic war, and by the time of the Russian surrender two-and-a-half years later, it had claimed over 200,000 lives, with the majority of the soldiers dying from infections.

By 1854, the financial situation at the Boly Mill was dire, and Francois couldn't compete with the local Lacade Mill, owned by the Mayor of Lourdes, which was modern and far better equipped. Francois even had to sell some of their furniture to pay the bills, but ultimately they couldn't continue to pay the rent and so they left their home at the Boly Mill on 24th June 1854, when Bernadette was ten.

This was a traumatic time for the family because it had been their home for over eleven years, but fortunately Claire Casterot came to the rescue and paid for the family to stay at the nearby Laborde House for a short period of time. Francois had to find work as a day labourer on very poor pay, while Louise found work doing domestic chores for various households and she also did labouring work on some farms in the area. Bernadette, being the eldest child had to help out at home with the chores and looking after her siblings, and by now she still hadn't attended school, although her sister Toinette was in the pauper's class of the local Hospice School in Lourdes.

The Soubirous family then moved into the Baudean Mill, but the poor wheat harvest and an inability to compete with the more efficient mills around them, made life very difficult. Louise gave birth to another boy, whom they named Justin, on 22nd February 1855, which meant that there were now four infants and children in the Soubirous family.

Bernadette contracted cholera during a pandemic that reached Lourdes in the autumn of 1855 and which killed 38 people in the town, and she was very fortunate to survive. But the high fevers caused her to be sickly thereafter, leaving her suffering from severe asthma and heart palpitations. In her weakened state she also developed tuberculosis of the bone. It may have been because of all her childhood illnesses and poor nutrition that Bernadette only grew to a height of 4 feet 7 inches.

In October 1855, Claire Casterot died and she left 900 francs to Louise and Francois, which they used to rent the Sarrabeyr House Mill at the nearby town of Arcizac-ez-Angles, East of Lourdes. However, the machinery in this mill was really old and inefficient and to make matters worse there'd been a very poor wheat harvest during the growing season earlier that year, so there wasn't enough wheat to grind to make the mill viable.

There was also a very severe winter at the end of 1855 and the Soubirous children all picked up bad colds and coughs as a result. When Bernarde Nicolau, the elder sister of Louise, visited the family in Arcizac one day, she was so shocked at the site of Bernadette coughing that she took her home to live with her for a while. In return, Bernadette helped with the chores in her Aunt Bernarde's house and she also looked after her little cousins as well.

As there was insufficient income from the mill to pay the rent, Francois was forced to take on various jobs as a day labourer in Lourdes, but the family quickly slipped into the depression of poverty. People who knew the Soubirous family could see the predicament that they were in, and some of them now began to shun the family, and there's no doubt that the 11 year old Bernadette would have been affected by all of this.

Within six months of moving into the mill at Arcizac, Francois was penniless once again and the family had to move out of the mill and into Rives House, which was described as being a 'miserable shack.' But by November 1856, the family was unable even to pay the small rental for this humble accomodation, and so they were soon evicted. Francois also suffered the humiliation of having to leave some of their last remaining items of furniture in lieu of the outstanding rent.

Fortunately the family was thrown a lifeline by a cousin named Andre Sajous, who allowed them to stay rent-free in a small room measuring about 4.4 metres by 4 metres, in a building that he owned. Andre and his family lived in the upper part of the same building. The room was described as being 'a foul and sombre hovel' and it had previously been used as a punishment cell or lock-up (Le Cachot), as it was part of the old jail which had been abandoned in 1824. At that time, the building had been condemned because it was 'unfit for human habitation'.

It's hard to imagine just how difficult it must have been for a family of six to have survived in such a confined space, and this is how Andre himself described conditions in Le Cachot: "The room was dark and in the backyard was the privy which overflowed and made the place stink. We kept the dung heap there. The Soubirous were destitute: two poor beds, one on the right as you entered, and the other on the same side nearer to the fireplace. They had only a little trunk to put all their linen in. My wife lent them some chemises: they were full of vermin. She often gave them a bit of bread made of millet. Yet the little ones never asked for anything. They would rather have starved."

At this time, Francois was working as a day labourer while Louise washed clothes for other families or worked as a farm-hand. In addition to looking after her siblings, Bernadette collected scraps of metal and bones which she then sold to a rag and bone merchant. Sometimes she also helped out in a tavern that was owned by her aunt.

On 27th March 1857, the Police went to the Cachot and arrested poor Francois on suspicion of having stolen two sacks of flour from the local Maissongrosse Bakery. Francois then had to endure the misery and embarrassment of spending eight long days in prison. He was finally released when the charges against him were dropped, although it still left some people in the town with the impression that he was a thief, which made it more difficult for him to find work as a labourer. The plaintiff later admitted, "It was his destitution that made me think that it could have been him."

The personal tragedies, poverty and hardships that the family faced didn't cause tensions and arguments as it would have done in many families, but instead it pulled them closer together, and Bernadette said that she'd never once heard her parents argue with each other.

The food shortages caused by successive wheat crop failures were so severe that Napoleon III eventually had to have bags of flour distributed to the poor of France. But throughout the misery of this period of time, the Soubirous family prayed together every morning and they also went to mass regularly. Francois and Louise taught the children how to pray the rosary, and the Our Father and Hail Mary prayers were the only French that Bernadette could speak. Andre recalled that he could hear the family praying the rosary together every single night and it was Bernadette who liked to lead the prayers.

On the Feast of Corpus Christi 1857, when all the other children of Bernadette's age were going up to the altar to receive Holy Communion, Bernadette began crying uncontrollably because she was unable to join them as she hadn't attended any catechism lessons. Louise must have felt terrible seeing her daughter in this state and it was probably one of the factors which prompted her to send Bernadette back to the village of Bartres in September of that year.

She was sent to the home of Marie Lagues, the lady who'd been her wet nurse, and here Bernadette looked after Marie's children and spent a lot of her time tending her sheep. But one of the main advantages of staying with Marie was that she could now attend catechism lessons on Sundays and also twice during the week. Her thoughtful sister, Toinette, had kindly bought Bernadette a rosary, which she carried around with her always and which she'd often recite by herself. It was a rosary which she would cherish for the rest of her life!

The fresh air in Bartres was good for Bernadette's health, but she still found herself exhausted at the end of each day, which made it difficult for her to concentrate when Marie taught her catechism at night. In fact by the age of thirteen, Bernadette still couldn't read or write, and she was the only girl in Lourdes who hadn't made her first communion by this age. Marie described Bernadette like this: "Bernadette, in spite of the tiredness which was caused by her shortness of breath and difficulty in breathing, always appeared happy and cheerful. She never gave us any trouble, she took what she was given, and appeared happy. We loved her very much as well."

But Bernadette soon became homesick and so she persuaded Marie to let her return to her family in Lourdes. She walked home by herself on 21st January 1858, two weeks after her 14th birthday, and despite the cramped conditions and poverty at Le Cachot, she was happy to be immersed in the love of her own family once again. Up until now, her bouts of sickness and the responsibility of looking after her siblings had prevented Bernadette from studying, but on returning to Lourdes she entered the hospice school run by the Sisters of Charity of Nevers, and as the family had no money she was placed in a pauper's class.

Bernadette regularly went to mass, but she had to just wait patiently in her pew and watch as her friends and other children from the town went up to receive Holy Communion. The catechism lessons were taught in French, and Bernadette needed to complete this course in order to make her own first communion, so she began learning how to read in a class full of 7 year old children. At this age she still couldn't speak French, but only spoke in the local dialect of that region of the Pyrenees. Father Pomian, the chaplain of the hospice, helped to prepare Bernadette for her first holy communion and it was this priest who heard her confessions and who would always stand by her.

Bernadette was sometimes teased by the other kids, who told her that she was stupid because of the way she struggled to learn, but she would just whisper that 'at least she would always know how to love the good God.' It was also difficult for Bernadette because people would make hurtful comments about the poor family living in Le Cachot. Jean Barbet was another teacher who taught Bernadette, and she had this to say about her: "Bernadette has difficulties retaining the words in Catechism which she cannot study because she does not know how to read. However, she applies enormous effort to comprehend the meaning of the explanations. She is very attentive, most especially she is very pious and modest."

Thursday 11th February 1858 was a typical, wet and cold winter's day, as Bernadette, her 11 year old sister Toinette, and a 12 year old friend of Bernadette named Jeanne Abadie went out to gather wood for the fire. Young Bernadette had no idea that this day would completely change the rest of her life, and that events over the next few months would rock the Catholic Church.

Chapter 2

Apparitions of Our Lady

First apparition

Thursday 11th February 1858

The three children walked down to the Pont-Vieux, which is a small stone bridge with two arches above the little river named Gave de Pau. They crossed over and then walked a few hundred metres further on, following the course of the canal which supplied water for the millstones of the local Savy Mill.

Bernadette asked Toinette and Jeanne if they wanted to see where the discharge water from the mill found its way back into the river, which they did. So they continued walking along until the canal rejoined the river and it was here that there was a large outcrop of rocks called masse vieille (old mass) or Massabielle. Pigs had grazed and foraged in the rough land around this site for over two centuries and at this time there were dozens of pigs there every night. Some locals also illegally put their cows out to pasture on this land at night as well, and so the whole area was in a filthy state, covered in animal hair and excrement.

Toinette and Jeanne took off their wooden shoes and began to walk through the shallow water of the stream to the other side. The girls said that the water was freezing cold, which made Bernadette anxious about having an asthma attack if she accidentally got her clothes wet. Bernadette then called out and asked them to throw some pebbles into the water to see how deep it was, so that she could find a shallow spot to walk over. But the two girls replied that the stream wasn't deep and that it was easy to cross, so Bernadette sat down to remove her shoes and stockings.

She'd just removed one stocking when she suddenly heard what sounded like a very strong gust of wind that seemed to have come from the direction of the rock face. Frightened by the noise, she stood up and looked around but was surprised to see that none of the wild shrubs or Poplar trees in the area were moving at all. As Bernadette began to remove her other stocking, she suddenly heard the loud noise once again, and this time when she looked over all she could see was a wild rosebush moving in a small cave in the cliff face.

It was then that Bernadette was shocked to see what looked like a cloud of golden coloured light coming from the cave, and as she stared at the entrance of the grotto, she then saw a lady dressed in white standing there.

The lady smiled at her and then motioned for Bernadette to come forward, but she was far too afraid to do so. The lady then raised her hands away from her body slightly, and it was then that Bernadette noticed that she had a rosary with large white beads on a golden chain draped over her right arm.

Although Bernadette later described herself as having been filled with fear at the time, she somehow felt an irresistible urge to stay where she was. Bernadette instinctively got down on her knees, took the rosary out of her pocket and tried to make the sign of the cross on her forehead, but was physically unable to raise her hand to her head.

She watched as the lady in the grotto made the sign of the cross herself, and after this Bernadette was able to do the same. Once she'd made the sign of the cross, Bernadette immediately felt all her fears disappear. Bernadette knelt down and began praying the rosary, and as she did so, she could see the lady moving the beads of her own rosary through her fingers, although her lips didn't appear to move at all.

After about 15 minutes, when she'd finished praying the rosary, Bernadette said that the lady motioned for her to come forward once again, but that she didn't dare do so. It was then that the lady simply disappeared and the golden light faded away at the same time.

After this apparition, the stunned Bernadette walked across the stream to join Toinette and Jeanne, who'd both noticed her kneeling on the ground as they collected some driftwood. Bernadette asked them if they'd seen anything unusual at the rock face, but they both replied that they hadn't seen anything at all. However, this immediately aroused their curiosity and so they kept on asking Bernadette if she'd seen something unusual while she was over there.

After they'd bundled up their horde of firewood, the girls decided to take a different route home, making the steep climb up the hillside behind the grotto. As they were walking along, Bernadette couldn't resist telling them about the astonishing thing that she'd just witnessed, and afterwards she asked them to keep it to themselves. Jeanne and

Toinette both told Bernadette that she shouldn't go back there again, and they said that they also wouldn't return to Massabielle just in case what Bernadette had seen would harm them.

Later at the Cachot while the family were saying their evening prayers, Bernadette's eyes started to well up with tears, which prompted Louise to ask her what was wrong. But before she could answer, Toinette excitedly told her parents that Bernadette had seen a lady dressed in white standing at the grotto earlier that day.

The news didn't go down well with her parents, with Francois showing his irritation at the whole story and with her mother dismissing what she thought she'd seen as being 'illusions.' Her parents also told her not to go back to Massabielle again.

It's no surprise that Bernadette found it impossible to sleep that night, because she couldn't shake the image of the beautiful lady from her mind, and despite what her parents had said, she knew that it hadn't been an illusion at all. No, the person that she'd seen that day had been very real indeed!

Bernadette later described the appearance of the lady at the grotto:

"She has the appearance of a young girl of sixteen and seventeen. She is dressed in a white robe, girdled at the waist with a blue ribbon which flows down all around it. A yoke closes it in graceful pleats at the base of the neck. The sleeves are long and tight-fitting. She wears upon her head a veil which is also white. This veil gives just a glimpse of her hair and then falls down at the back below her waist. Her feet are bare but covered by the last folds of her robe except at the point where a yellow rose shines upon each of them. She holds on her right arm a rosary of white beads with a chain of gold shining like the two roses on her feet." On another occasion, Bernadette said that the lady had blue eyes.

Bernadette later confessed to Father Pomian that she'd seen an apparition at the grotto, and at that time he just put it down to her playful imagination. However he did suggest that she should tell the Parish Priest about what she thought she'd seen.

She replied, "I'd rather you did, Father!"

Father Pomian did in fact discuss the matter with Father Peyramale, but he just dismissed the issue out of hand.

Second apparition

Sunday 14th February 1858

Although Bernadette had been asked by her parents not to go back to the grotto, she felt a strong internal compulsion to return there that Sunday. So after High Mass that morning she pleaded with her parents to change their minds. Francois eventually said, "A lady with a Rosary can't be evil," and so in the end they allowed her to go back.

So Bernadette, Toinette, Jeanne and some others made their way to Massabielle, following the same route the girls had taken home the previous Thursday, coming down from the cliff above the grotto. This time Bernadette had taken a vial of holy water with her, which she intended to sprinkle near the apparition if it did appear to her again.

Standing near the grotto at the base of the rock face, Bernadette began to recite the rosary, and as she finished the first decade, the children noticed that her facial expression had completely changed. The apparition had appeared once again, but as was the case on the previous Thursday, only Bernadette could see it.

She threw some of the holy water in the direction of the apparition and said that if she was from God then she should stay, otherwise she should go away. The lady then smiled at Bernadette, moved forward a little and bowed her head. Toinette, Jeanne and the others were looking on, but could see nothing at the grotto except Bernadette, who was now in a strange trance-like state.

Suddenly gripped by fear, they all ran off for help from Madame Nicolau, whose family owned the nearby Savy Mill. Madame Nicolau rushed to the grotto with her son Antoine, and when they arrived there, they both witnessed Bernadette in a state of ecstasy. Antoine had to use all his strength to lift Bernadette off the ground, because despite her tiny size, she'd somehow become like a dead weight. Antoine carried her back to the mill and later said that he'd never seen anything in his whole life so beautiful as Bernadette was when she was in that ecstatic state.

Bernadette later said that on the way to the Savy Mill, she could see the lady in front and slightly above her, and that the apparition only disappeared when Antoine carried her inside the mill.

Toinette then rushed home to the Cachot and poured out the whole story to her mother, who, in a panic ran all the way over to Massabielle herself. When Louise saw her daughter at the Savy mill she began crying with relief that she was okay, but distressed by the whole ordeal she snapped at Bernadette, "You are making everyone run after you!"

It didn't take long for news of this apparition to filter throughout the whole town of Lourdes, with the townsfolk having all sorts of interpretations as to who or what had caused it. Initially Louise banned Bernadette from going near the grotto ever again, but an influential lady named Madame Millet somehow convinced Louise to allow her to go back to Massabielle, if Bernadette was accompanied by herself and her seamstress, Antoinette Peyret. Antoinette and some others thought that the apparition may have been the soul of a person who'd died in Lourdes, who'd now returned to earth from Purgatory.

Third Apparition

Thursday 18th February 1858

Bernadette, Madame Millet and Antoinette Peyret went to early morning mass together that day, before making their way down to Massabielle, with Madame Millet holding a blessed candle for their spiritual protection. When they reached the grotto, they started to pray the rosary together and it was then that Bernadette saw the lady, who she referred to as 'Aquero' once again. This time the lady actually came down and stood next to her, but again no-one except Bernadette could see the apparition.

Antoinette had sensibly brought along a pen, some paper and ink, and she suggested that Bernadette ask the apparition to write down her name or any requests that she might have. So Bernadette asked this of the lady, who replied, "There is no need for me to write what I have to say to you. Would you have the graciousness to come here for fifteen days?"

Bernadette was stunned that the lady spoke to her in the local patois and also that she was so gracious towards her.

She answered, "I will ask my parents permission, and I will come."

The lady then said, "I do not promise to make you happy in this life, but in the next."

The apparition then said to her, **"Go and tell the priests that a chapel must be built here."**

Bernadette said that the lady's eyes then rested on Antoinette for a moment and that she smiled once again before disappearing.

Fourth apparition
Friday 19th February 1858

After some agonisng and debate, Bernadette's parents decided to allow her to continue visiting the grotto each day and so early on the Friday morning Bernadette went to the grotto with seven other people, including her Aunt Bernarde, her mother Louise and some neighbours. She was given a blessed candle to hold for her protection.

All seven of these people witnessed the look on her face changing and becoming incredibly peaceful as she was in ecstasy, which moved her mother deeply, and she said to the others, "Who is it that she sees?"

At one point Louise feared that Bernadette might even die because of the serene and ecstatic state that she was in and so she prayed, "O God, do not take my child away from me."

When the apparition vanished, Bernadette immediately hugged her mother and said, "The Lady thanked me for coming. She told me she would have some revelations to make to me."

Fifth apparition
Saturday 20th February 1858

Bernadette went to the grotto early in the morning with her Aunt Lucille, her mother Louise and about thirty other people from Lourdes. They all stood and watched Bernadette at prayer but they couldn't see the apparition or hear what the lady said to her.

It was on this day that the lady gave Bernadette a personal prayer to recite each day, which she never made public, but which she said every day for the rest of her life. The lady also asked her to always bring a candle that had been blessed, along with her to the grotto.

The small crowd walked back to the town completely stunned by the serenity and joy that they'd all felt at the grotto that morning.

Father Pene, who was the priest responsible for the local district, asked Bernadette about the happiness she felt while praying at the grotto and she replied, "When I see her I feel as if I'm no longer of this world. And when the vision disappears I'm amazed to find myself still here."

Father Pene always believed in the sincerity of Bernadette and that she had indeed witnessed an apparition, and he would later defend her cause when other clergy in the church doubted her.

Sixth apparition

Sunday 21st February 1858

By now word was spreading fast about the apparitions and well over a hundred people descended on Massabielle on that Sunday. This is how Bernadette recalled the sixth apparition:

"Sunday was the Lady's sixth visit to me. Hundreds of people were kneeling by the grotto, but I scarcely noticed them. The light around the Lady was brighter, yet softer than the sun. The roses on her feet were brighter than gold.

"For a moment she looked out over my head, and sorrow overshadowed her. I asked her 'why?'

"She answered, '**Pray for sinners**.'

"She was surrounded by light as she disappeared, the glow faded, but its warmth lingered in my soul."

While Bernadette was in a state of ecstasy, a local and respected physician named Doctor Dozou, walked right up to Bernadette and took her pulse. He was surprised that despite her trancelike state, her breathing and heart rate were completely normal and he informed the crowd of this.

The commotion at Massabielle had by now drawn the attention of the local police, who came down and counted the number of people in the crowd that day. Many of the residents of Lourdes were becoming anxious about this situation as well and so they convened a meeting to discuss the whole affair with the public officials. Some believed that Bernadette had genuinely seen something supernatural, but many were unconvinced, and in the end they put pressure on Jacques Vital Dutour, the Public Prosecutor, to ban Bernadette from ever returning to the grotto.

Dutour was convinced that Bernadette had been suffering hallucinations at the grotto and agreed that she shouldn't go back there. However Bernadette bravely told Dutour that she couldn't give her word that she wouldn't return to Massabielle because she had already said to the lady at the grotto that she'd return there every day. The frustrated Public Prosecutor asked her to leave the room and then took the matter up with Dominique Jacomet, the Police Commissioner and with Jean-Baptiste Estrade, who was an official from the local Tax Office.

Early that evening, as she was leaving church after Vespers (sunset hour prayers), Jacomet walked over to Bernadette, grabbed her by the hood and said sharply, "Follow me!"

Jacomet then marched her to his home, where he vigorously and unsympathetically questioned her in his office. The Commissioner wrote down all her answers on a sheet of paper with a goose quill, and at the end of his interrogation he read all her answers back to her.

But Jacomet had distorted many of her replies and so Bernadette argued with him over this for a long time, refusing to change the original answers that she'd given to him.

At one point he asked her, "So, then, Bernadette, you see this Holy Virgin?"

But Bernadette just replied, "I do not say that I have seen the Holy Virgin."

To which the Commissioner exclaimed, "Ah, good! You haven't seen anything!"

But Bernadette, young and uneducated as she was, wasn't going to be intimidated by this and she replied, "Yes, I did see something."

"Well what did you see?" Jacomet asked in frustration.

Bernadette replied, "Something white."

"Something or someone?" he asked.

Bernadette answered, "Aquero has the form of a young lady."

Fortunately some of the church goers who'd attended Vespers had seen Bernadette being led away and they'd followed her to the Police Commissioner's home. It didn't take long before a crowd started gathering outside his house, which was becoming increasingly agitated and vocal the longer she was being detained by him.

Bernadette was questioned for over an hour, towards the end of which she could hear the Commissioner's front door being kicked and the shutters of the windows bashed by some people in the crowd. At one point the crowd started pushing her father, Francois forward, telling him to demand that his daughter be released. Then, to Bernadette's great relief, Francois walked into Jacomet's office and said, "I am the father of this little one!"

The Police Commissioner could see that emotions were now running high and so he reluctantly allowed Bernadette to leave, but he first demanded an assurance from Francois that he would ban his daughter from returning to the grotto and that the disturbances would cease. Poor Francois was always uncomfortable being in the presence of officials, not least because he'd previously been accused of stealing two sacks of flour for which he served eight days in prison. In 1857 he'd also been charged with the theft of a wooden beam, which he thought had been thrown away.

Understandably, Bernadette was deeply upset by these events, but her mother Louise defended her by saying of her daughter, "She is no liar!"

Monday 22nd February 1858

Bernadette went off to school as usual this Monday morning, but had to endure a hostile reception from the other girls, as well as some of the sisters. The Sister Superior even thanked God that Bernadette had been arrested the previous night and another woman came up and slapped her across the face.

Bernadette did her best to ignore all this hostility while she was in the classroom that morning. However, later in the day, just after she'd finished eating her lunch and was on her way back to her class for the next lesson, she felt an irresistible pull to return to the grotto.

She was now caught in a moral dilemma and so she went home and then said to her mother and father, "I must disobey you or Aquero."

In the end, Bernadette decided to ignore the Police Commissioner's warning and so she made her way down to the grotto, followed by a policeman and a small crowd of people. As she walked, the policeman made sarcastic comments to her about how strange it was that people still believed in religion despite the fact that they were now living in an age of scientific advancement.

On reaching the grotto she knelt down to pray the rosary as she always did, with people watching her every move, but this time the apparition didn't appear. When Bernadette finally got to her feet, the policeman asked her if she'd seen anything and she replied, "No, this time I saw nothing at all."

Bernadette started to walk home, but was mocked as she went, with some people openly threatening her. Others taunted her by saying that perhaps the lady hadn't appeared that day because she was scared of the police, and that she must have found a safer place to go.

She was obviously feeling bad about defying the authorities by continuing to go to the grotto, because that evening she went to see Father Pomain, the assistant priest who always heard her confessions. But he reassured her that it was okay for her to continue going because Dutour, the Public Prosecutor hadn't actually banned her from going back, only the Police Commissioner, and it was only Dutour that really had the authority to impose a ban.

Seventh apparition

Tuesday 23rd February 1858

Bernadette and her mother left for Massabielle very early in the morning hoping to avoid the crowds, but when they arrived there they found a large group of about 150 people already waiting for Bernadette. Some prominent people from the town had even made the effort to walk there, including Jean-Baptiste Estrade, the excise tax official, and Doctor Dozous. Some wealthy individuals had come purely out of curiosity and many of them had been scathing of the way in which the working class people had been behaving at the grotto.

Father Peyramale, who was by this stage also curious about what was happening at Massabielle, had asked Estrade to go there that morning and to give him some feedback on what he saw there.

The lady again appeared to Bernadette that morning, and this time she saw the apparition for about an hour, during which time Bernadette was seen to periodically bow down low to the ground.

At times she looked serious and appeared to be listening very attentively to what was being said to her, and at other times she appeared utterly joyful. Bernadette later said that the Lady had prayed with her for that hour and that she was surprised that no-one else could hear the lady speaking.

When the crowd witnessed the countenance of Bernadette's face change while she was in ecstasy, they were deeply shocked and the men immediately took off their hats and fell to their knees. Bernadette felt a deep sadness when the Lady disappeared, but she took comfort when she realised that Louise had been kneeling right beside her all along.

Even Estrade was convinced that Bernadette was looking at something supernatural right in front of her. So now, even the most hardened cynics in the crowd that day had come to believe that she was telling the truth about these visions. As with Saul on the road to Damascus, the leading men of the town had themselves become witnesses!

When asked later what the lady had said to her, Bernadette replied that three revelations had been given to her, but she never made any of these public.

Eighth apparition

Wednesday 24th February 1858

Francois, Louise and Bernadette's aunt, Lucille, all accompanied Bernadette to the grotto that day. About three hundred people that had gathered between the River Gave and the grotto watched in stunned silence as tears streamed down Bernadette's transfigured face while she was in a state of ecstasy.

Bernadette later said that she couldn't take her eyes off the radiant presence of the apparition. She also said that the Lady had repeated slowly and deliberately and with great sadness three times over:

"Repentance, Repentance, Repentance."

Bernadette's eyes filled with tears as she repeated the words slowly, just as the Lady had said them, and the crowd all heard it and began saying it themselves.

After Bernadette finished praying the rosary, she lay face down on the ground and kissed it, and she repeated this devotion several times over.

Lucille was standing there in tears watching, and Bernadette later told her that the Lady had said:

"Pray to God for the conversion of sinners."

The stunned crowd continued to repeat the word 'Repentance' as they walked back in the winter sunshine towards the town.

Ninth apparition

Thursday 25th February 1858

A crowd of about 350 had gathered in the misty, wet weather very early this Thursday morning before Bernadette arrived at the grotto. When she got there, they watched in silence as she bent down and kissed the ground several times as she'd done the day before, as an act of penance for sinners.

She then put her candle down and removed her hood before walking away from the grotto towards the river. Everyone was wondering what she was doing as she then crawled on her hands and knees all the way back to the grotto, before scratching at the ground with her bare hands. The crowd then witnessed Bernadette holding her cupped hands up to her face a few times and she also rubbed some muddy earth all over her face and even ate some of the grass that was growing there. The crowd was absolutely horrified when Bernadette then stood up and turned towards them, with her face covered in mud, still chewing on the grass. Some were so disturbed by her behaviour that they began to think that she was insane, but others became angry and resentful, and many of the people who'd begun to believe in Bernadette now turned their backs on her.

Bernadette's Aunt Bernarde even slapped her in the face and said, "Stop your nonsense!" before marching her off home, but as she walked past the crowd Bernadette had to endure all their glares and insults.

Bernadette explained later that the Lady had gently said to her, "Go, drink at the spring, and wash in it." But she'd been confused by this because there was no spring there at the time, which is why she initially went towards the river. Bernadette said that it was at this point that the Lady had called her back and then indicated with her finger where to look for the spring.

Bernadette said that as she scratched at the ground, she'd noticed that the earth was becoming moist and that a small pool was forming with bubbles rising in it. She had then collected some of the muddy water in her hands and tried to drink it, but had to throw it away three times because it was more mud than water. However on the fourth attempt she'd managed to swallow the water from her cupped hands. Bernadette also said that after she'd drunk the water, the apparition had just disappeared.

A few people who witnessed the events that Thursday realised that something deeply significant had just happened at the grotto that morning. One of those was a lady named Marie Pailhes, who was completely overcome with emotion at the pitiful state of Bernadette. Marie later described how Bernadette looked, saying, "She seemed to carry all the sorrow of the world!"

Estrade wrote that the 25th February had been "An unforgettably gloomy day" and he and many other leading men of the town were angry that they'd been taken in by this 'hoax,' with some saying that Bernadette was no more than a 'filthy little upstart.'

However, curiosity drove some people who'd been present in the crowd that morning back to Massabielle later that afternoon. Bernadette also returned there with a lady named Eleanore Perard and at the place where she'd been scraping the ground earlier that day, she found the hole still bubbling up with water. The people standing there were amazed that the hole didn't dry up despite many of them taking water from it. Some of the people in the crowd who'd mocked Bernadette earlier on, now saw the spring as a gift from God and drank the water from it themselves.

There was a man named Louis Bouriette living in Lourdes who'd suffered a very serious injury to his right eye caused by an explosion while working as a labourer in the quarry in 1839. His brother Joseph had been killed right next to him during the same incident.

Louis had very nearly died as well, but he was eventually nursed back to good health, apart from his irreparably damaged eye. Despite Doctor Dozous's treatments over the years, the eyesight of his right eye continued to worsen and by 1856 he could no longer distinguish between a man standing in front of him and a tree at the same distance.

Louis had heard about the spring that had appeared at Massabielle and so he said to his daughter, "Go and get me some of that water. The Blessed Virgin, if it be her, has only to wish it, and I shall be cured."

When she arrived back half an hour later, he bathed his eye in the muddy water repeatedly as he prayed to the Virgin Mary. Louis then let out a shout of joy and started trembling as he began to see again through his right eye. He continued praying and bathing his eye in the water a few more times until his sight was completely restored.

It's surely no coincidence that the Gospel reading at Mass that very morning was about Jesus healing a man who'd been blind since birth.

John 9:7: "Go," he told him, "Wash in the Pool of Siloam." So the man went and washed, and came home seeing.

At 6pm that Thursday evening, poor Bernadette was called to give an account of herself before Dutour, the Public Prosecutor, and the mood in his home could not have been more hostile. Fortunately Louise was with Bernadette throughout the two hour interrogation, during which time various false accusations were made against her. Dutour, pompously sitting beneath a picture of Napoleon III, demanded to know what had been happening at the grotto, and as she answered the questions, he wrote down all her answers.

He then read her replies back to her, but Bernadette denied having said some of the things that he'd just written down. Dutour then said that he had Police Commissioner Jacomet's report from her prior interview on his desk, and that what she was now saying had happened at the grotto differed from Jacomet's report.

Dutour then said that he was going to have Bernadette and her mother imprisoned for the night, and so he sent someone to ask the Police Superintendant and an official from the prison to come to his house. Louise had been crying sporadically during the interrogation, but when she heard that they were about to spend the night in prison, it was too much for her and she broke down in tears.

Bernadette and her mother had been standing throughout the entire grilling, and it was only when Louise looked as though she were about to faint that Dutour asked for two chairs to be brought into the room. Louise, who was trembling nervously, sat down, but Bernadette defiantly refused, saying, "No thanks, I might dirty it!" and she sat down on the floor instead.

By this time a crowd had gathered outside the house and in the crowd was Bernadette's cousin, Andrew Sajous, who banged on the shutters of Dutour's windows. Some of the men also started kicking his front door, shouting for Bernadette to be released. Dutour opened the window a few times and told them to be quiet, but the crowd became increasingly agitated and in the end he released them both to prevent the situation from getting out of hand.

Friday 26th February 1858

Bernadette returned to the grotto exhausted from the events the previous night, but she didn't see the apparition on this day. However by then a lot of water was coming from the hole in the ground where she'd been digging. Some scoffed and said that there must always have been water in the grotto, but those who were honest knew full well that there'd never been a spring there before.

This same day, Louis Bouriette saw Doctor Dozous walking in the street and went running up to him, shouting, "I am cured! I am cured!"

"Impossible!" the doctor replied. "You have an organic affection which makes your disease absolutely incurable. The treatment which I made you follow was only to ease your pain; it could not restore your sight!"

But Louis responded, "It is not you who has cured me. It is the Blessed Virgin of the grotto!" Louis then went on to explain that he'd bathed his eye in water from the spring at Massabielle and that his eyesight had immediately returned.

Dozous looked at Louis and said, "That Bernadette has ecstasies which cannot be explained, is certain; I have verified that myself. But that the water which gushed forth from the grotto from some unknown cause, suddenly cures incurable diseases, is not possible."

To prove his point, the doctor took out a little memorandum book and wrote on it with a pencil without Louis being able to see what he was writing: "Bouriette has an incurable amaurosis, and he will never be cured."

By then a small group of passers-by, curious to see what was going on, had gathered around the two men. Dozous then covered Louis' left eye, held the paper up to his injured right eye and said to him, "If you can read this I will believe you."

To his astonishment, Louis then read the words back perfectly. Dr Dozous asked him how it was possible that his sight had been restored, and Louis again explained that he'd bathed his eye in water from the grotto. The doctor was visibly shaken by what he'd just seen, and said, "I cannot deny it. It is a miracle, a real miracle, without disparagement to myself and to my brothers of the Faculty. "I am amazed; but the fact is evident; it is beyond all that poor human science can do!"

What was remarkable about the case of Louis Bouriette is that the terrible scarring and damage of the eye still remained after his healing, and yet he could now see perfectly with it.

Tenth apparition

Saturday 27th February 1858

On this day, Bernadette again saw the apparition and she held a blessed candle in her hand throughout. She said that the lady had once again said to her, **"Kiss the ground on behalf of sinners,"** so Bernadette kissed the ground and remarkably, so did the crowd who'd gathered at the grotto to watch her. It was also on this morning that Father Peyramale met with his three curates to advise them of his personal thoughts on the reported apparitions. This is what he said, according to Jean Baptiste Estrade:

"You have heard the reports which are going about respecting certain appearances which are supposed to have taken place in a Grotto near the Gave. I don't know how much is truth and how much is fancy in the current legend, but it is our duty as Priests to maintain the greatest reserve in matters of this nature. If the appearances are genuine and of a divine character God will let us know it in his own time. If they are illusions or caused by the spirit of lies, God has no need of our intervention to reveal the falsehood.

"It would therefore be rash of us to show ourselves at present at the Grotto. If the visions are recognised as genuine later on, we shall certainly be accused of bringing about this recognition by our own machinations. If they are subsequently rejected as without foundation, we shall be ridiculed for what will be called our disappointment. So we must not take any unconsidered step or speak any rash word; the interests of religion and of our own dignity are concerned. The present circumstances demand of us the greatest circumspection."

Eleventh apparition

Sunday 28th February 1858

Well over a thousand people descended on Massabielle this day, and by now curious people from the surrounding villages were pouring into Lourdes as well. Bernadette saw the apparition once again and she kissed the ground at the grotto on behalf of sinners. Many people in the crowd held burning candles in front of them while Bernadette was in a state of ecstasy and some left them burning at the grotto long after Bernadette had left.

A magistrate named Judge Clement Ribes who happened to be on a visit to Lourdes, took it upon himself to call poor Bernadette in for questioning. For whatever reason, perhaps because he'd discussed the matter with Jacques Dutour, this magistrate then tried to get her to recant her comments about what she'd seen and heard at the grotto, but she refused to do so. Judge Ribes also put pressure on Bernadette to immediately cease her daily visits to the grotto, but she ignored all his threats and continued going there as the lady had asked her to do.

Twelfth apparition

Monday 1ˢᵗ March 1858

On this day, Bernadette went to the grotto holding the rosary of a friend of hers named Pauline Sans, who'd asked her to do so. Bernadette later said that the Lady had interrupted her by saying, "You have made a mistake. That Rosary is not yours."

Bernadette said that the lady kept smiling on the people in the crowd and she could see that the lady loved them and that she always seemed sorry to leave.

The crowd that day was about 1500 strong and the priests at St Pierre's were absolutely shocked at the number of people who were being converted after having seen Bernadette in a state of ecstasy at the grotto. The churches were now full at mass times and people were eagerly queuing up each day to confess their sins.

Father Peyramale's ban on the clergy visiting the grotto was still in place so that no-one could say that the Church was in any way endorsing what Bernadette claimed was happening there. However there was a visiting priest in town that day named Father Desirat, who was probably unaware of Father Peyramale's instruction, and he was standing close to Bernadette when she saw the apparition and fell into a state of ecstasy.

Later that day Father Desirat wrote down his thoughts: "What struck me was the joy, the sadness reflected in Bernadette's face - Respect, silence, recollection reigned everywhere. Oh it was good to be there. It was like being at the gates of paradise."

It was also on this day that another miracle occurred at the grotto. A 39 year old lady named Catherine Latapie-Chouat, who lived in the nearby town of Loubajac, had a sudden impulse in the middle of the night to go to the grotto. Two of the fingers of Catherine's right hand had been completely paralysed since she injured her arm falling out of a tree in October 1856.

She got up at 3am and made the four mile walk to Lourdes with her two young children, despite the fact that she was nine months pregnant at the time. She arrived at dawn, where she saw Bernadette already standing at the grotto. Catherine later went up to the pool at the back of the cave and immersed her arm in it and she spontaneously regained the full use of her hand.

She then made the long walk back home and gave birth to a baby boy within a few minutes of opening her front door. They named their son Jean-Baptiste, and he would later be ordained a priest in 1882. This miracle, along with several others that happened in 1858, would only be officially recognisd by the Church four years later.

Thirteenth Apparition

Tuesday 2nd March 1858

Once more Bernadette made her way to the grotto early in the morning, and when she got there she took out her rosary and began to pray, quickly falling into an ecstatic state in front of the huge crowd that had gathered.

Before the lady disappeared, Bernadette heard her say, "**Go and tell the priests to build a chapel here and to have people come in procession.**"

So Bernadette went with her Aunt Basile to Father Peyramale to deliver the message of the lady. Peyramale was actually a kind hearted man, but his generous nature was hidden beneath a tough façade, and so many of the parishioners were a little wary of him. In fact he cared deeply for the poor and had even paid the rents of many families in the town to prevent them from being evicted by their landlords.

As Bernadette began to make the request about the procession known, the priest became irritated with her, called her an imposter and a show-off and sent her away, warning her not to go back to the grotto. She hadn't even had time to mention the chapel that the lady said should be built there.

Bernadette burst into tears and left with her aunt, but the 47 year old priest underestimated the steely resolve of this 14 year old girl, and to his surprise she returned to the presbytery to give him the message again that night.

Peyramale had perhaps realised by now that he'd been too harsh with her, or else he'd been reflecting on the whole issue, and so this time he didn't chase her off straight away. But after hearing what Bernadette had to say about the Lady's request for a chapel to be built, he started pacing up and down and said, "A chapel, a chapel! Who will pay for it? And if your Lady wants processions, she should send you to the Bishop, not to me. You don't even know her name. Ridiculous!"

The priest then picked up a broom that was standing nearby and motioned with it as though he were sweeping her away, and so Bernadette quickly left for home.

However, Father Peyramale was now becoming concerned about this whole situation at the grotto and wanted direction on how to proceed from his superiors, and so he went through to discuss it all with Monsignor Laurence, who was the Bishop in Tarbes.

Bishop Laurence thought it wise for Father Peyramale to continue to stay away from Massabielle, despite the thousands of people who were now visiting the site.

Fourteenth apparition
Wednesday 3rd March 1858

A crowd of over three thousand had gathered at the grotto the next morning, but Bernadette didn't see the apparition at that time. However, when she returned in the evening, she saw the lady once again, although only for a brief period.

On this occasion the lady again greeted Bernadette and bowed to her before making the Sign of the Cross. She again asked for a chapel to be built by the clergy and said that the people should come to this chapel in a procession.

Bernadette said that when the lady disappeared, she was amazed to find herself still in this world, which just shows how detached she was from everything around her while in a state of ecstasy.

Bernadette decided to put her fear of Father Peyramale to one side and she went back to him with the lady's requests again later that evening.

The priest didn't hide is frustration as he said, "Well, if she wants her chapel, let her tell her name, and let her make the rosebush blossom. Then I will build the chapel, and if I build it, I tell you, it will not be a small one."

Fifteenth apparition
Thursday 4th March 1858

By now, news of Bernadette's visions at Massabielle had reached most parts of the country, and it was well known that this day marked the last day of the 15 days that the lady had asked Bernadette to visit the grotto. There was a growing expectation that the lady might reveal her name or even perform some wonderful miracle on this day.

About 8000 people gathered at the grotto to pray, although some estimates put the figure much higher than this, with some of them having prayed there throughout the night. The civil authorities had even inspected the grotto before Bernadette arrived, to make sure that no-one had tampered with the site in some way by planting something that could then be used as evidence of a miracle. There was also a police presence at the grotto and a contingent of soldiers was there to ensure that the situation didn't get out of control.

Bernadette arrived with Jeanne Vedere, her cousin, just after 7 am, guarded by two soldiers who were armed with swords. A path was cleared for Bernadette, who seemed completely oblivious to all the commotion around her. She got down on the ground to pray the Rosary and fell into a state of ecstasy once again, moving around the grotto on her knees.

The crowd was respectful and silent as they watched Bernadette in this state for about an hour, with Jeanne right beside her. Bernadette later said that the lady was so close to Jeanne that had she just reached out her hand, she could have touched the lady.

But when Bernadette rose from prayer after the lady had disappeared, there'd been no further revelations and the rosebush hadn't miraculously bloomed, which left many in the crowd disappointed and disillusioned. However Bernadette told the onlookers that the lady hadn't indicated to her on this visit that she wouldn't be returning to the grotto ever again.

Bernadette then walked back to Le Cachot deep in thought, followed by a large crowd who wanted to see her up close, to touch her or to ask her questions about what she'd just experienced. Some people prayed in the streets on their knees and a few of them even went inside her tiny home, hoping to be given a souvenir. Although her family was desperately poor, she refused the money that some people tried to put in her hands.

Bernadette went to see Father Peyramale again, saying that when she'd asked the lady for her name as he'd requested of her, that the lady had just smiled.

Peyramale then said firmly, "She must tell her name!"

But what the priest said next really surprised Bernadette, because it showed that deep down he wasn't as dismissive of what she'd been saying all along as he appeared to be. He said quietly, "If I knew it was the Blessed Virgin, I would do all she desires."

5th to 24th March 1858

After the life-changing and tempestuous events of the last two weeks, Bernadette returned to school, where she started learning how to read and write and to speak in French, and she also attended catechism lessons so that she could make her First Holy Communion.

Every day after she finished her lessons she would make her way down to Massabielle where she'd kneel down, make the Sign of the Cross just as the Lady had taught her, and then say her prayers. Crowds of people still made their way to the grotto each day as well, with many of them carrying candles or flowers to leave at the site and they openly prayed in front of it.

On Thursday 18th March, Bernadette was called in to be questioned about the various miracles that had been reported after people had visited the grotto, and they also asked what her future plans were regarding visiting the site.

Some officials in the town still thought that Bernadette was delusional and so she was also subjected to three examinations by doctors to determine whether she was in a fit mental state. All three physicians agreed that there was nothing wrong with the fourteen year old girl, except for her severe asthma.

The police were also impressed by Bernadette's composure and sincerity during their own questioning throughout this time, but most of the clergy remained sceptical of the whole affair.

Sixteenth apparition

Thursday 25ᵗʰ March 1858

On this day, Bernadette awoke at four in the morning with an irresistible compulsion to go straight to the grotto, but her parents wouldn't allow her to leave the house until an hour later.

Bernadette later said that when she arrived at Massabielle it was still dark, but that the lady was already standing there. Bernadette apologised for having kept her waiting and the lady just smiled at her.

Bernadette then knelt down, fell into a state of ecstasy and began praying the Rosary in unison with the lady. After she'd finished praying, the lady came up very close to Bernadette and it was then that she told the lady just how much she loved her and how happy she was to see her again.

Bernadette then asked, "Mademoiselle, would you be so kind as to tell me who you are, if you please?"

Bernadette said that the lady didn't reply, but just smiled at her once again. After this she asked the same question two more times without receiving a reply. However, when she asked the Lady a fourth time, she did receive an answer - one that would shock the Christian world.

Bernadette later said, "The Lady extended her hands towards the ground, swept them upwards to join them on her heart, raised her eyes, but not her head to Heaven, leaned tenderly towards me and said, **'Que soy era Immaculada Conceptiou.'**

After the Lady had said this, she smiled at Bernadette and disappeared.

The words were spoken in her local Bigourdan dialect, and in English they translate as, **"I am the Immaculate Conception."**

After the Apparition disappeared, Bernadette placed a candle at the grotto to thank the lady for the revelation that she'd just received.

Bernadette later said, "I did not understand the words, but I knew the priest would. I knew also the lady loved the priest. Leaving my candle at the grotto, I went straight to Father Peyramale, saying the lady's name to myself along the way.

"Father was waiting for me. I bowed and said, 'I am the Immaculate Conception.' Seeing his surprise, I explained, 'Aquero said, "I am the Immaculate Conception."'

"The good Priest stood there stunned. Suddenly he stammered, 'Do you know what that means?'

"I shook my head, I said 'No'.

"He said, 'Then how can you say the words if you do not understand them?'

"'I repeated them all along the way,' I replied, then added, 'She still wants the chapel.'

"The Priest by now was deathly pale, but he pulled himself together, saying, 'Go home now child. I will see you another day.'"

Father Peyramale wrote to Monsignor Laurence in Tarbes that same day to inform him of what Bernadette had just said. One of the comments he made in his letter was, "She could never have invented this."

It's not surprising that the priest was shocked on hearing what Bernadette had said, and he was quite correct in writing what he did to the bishop, because at that time Bernadette could still not read or write.

The doctrine of the Immaculate Conception had only been proclaimed infallible by Pope Pius IX in the bull titled "**Ineffabilis Deus**" in 1854, after consulting with the 603 bishops in the Church.

"We declare, pronounce and define that the doctrine which holds that the Blessed Virgin Mary, at the first instant of her conception, by a singular privilege and grace of the Omnipotent God, in virtue of the merits of Jesus Christ, the Saviour of mankind, was preserved immaculate from all stain of original sin, has been revealed by God, and therefore should firmly and constantly be believed by all the faithful." Pope Pius IX, Ineffabilis Deus, 1854.

Some people confuse the conception of Jesus in the womb of the Virgin Mary by the Holy Spirit with this teaching. But the Immaculate Conception actually refers to the conception of the Virgin Mary herself in her mother Anne's body.

It's surely no coincidence that it was on this specific day that the Lady announced to Bernadette exactly who she was! After all, the 25th March in the Catholic Church is the feast date of the Annunciation, which commemorates the day that the angel Gabriel announced to the Virgin Mary that She would carry the Christ in her womb. This feast has been celebrated since the 4th or 5th century, and its first definitive mention is in a canon from the Council of Toledo which convened in 656 AD.

Later that evening, she asked Mademoiselle Estrade to explain what the words meant and it was only then that she was told that the Virgin Mary had been given that title.

Bernadette later said, "It was then I realised I could speak what was unspoken in my soul for seven silent weeks – that Aquero was the Immaculate Virgin Mary. She was the Mother of God, and she had been stepping out of Heaven to share her soul with me. She had taught me prayers no soul on earth had prayed. She had promised me happiness, not in this world, but in the next."

And it wasn't just Father Peyramale who was in a state of shock, because the news that the Lady had said that she was the 'Immaculate Conception' had stunned everyone in Lourdes, and news of this spread quickly throughout the whole of France.

Bernadette was then subjected to further questioning and she was examined by three doctors who all found that she was mentally and emotionally stable. On one occasion she was asked by a politician what language the Virgin Mary had used when she addressed her at the grotto.

Bernadette simply replied, "She spoke to me in dialect."

The politician who was questioning her then scornfully responded by saying, "The Blessed Virgin could not have spoken in patois. God and the Blessed Virgin don't know that language."

But Bernadette innocently responded, "How can we know and speak dialect if they don't speak it? Do you think she spoke to me in French? Do I speak French?"

Another miracle was also reported in March 1858 and it involved a fifty year old lady named Blaisette Cazenave. She'd been suffering for many years from a chronic infection of the conjunctivae and eyelids, which had impaired her vision and resulted in fleshy outgrowths all around her eyelids. Blaisette's physician had declared that her condition was incurable after having tried for many years to improve it.

Blaisette placed some water from the grotto in her eyes on two occasions, and on the second application her eyelids returned to normal, with the growths disappearing and the inflammation subsiding completely.

Professor Vergez later wrote: "The supernatural effect was as much evident in this wonderful cure as the physical lesion – nowadays we would say the organic disease of the eyelids – striking as that was, with the complete return to a normal healthy state by a rapid regrowth of the tissues."

Seventeenth apparition

Wednesday 7th April 1858

On this Wednesday Bernadette felt an inner call to visit the grotto again and so she walked down there holding her blessed candle. Bernadette fell to her knees to pray the rosary and immediately fell into a state of ecstasy in front of the silent crowd that had gathered there. But this meeting was different because she knew without any shadow of doubt that she was kneeling in the presence of the Mother of Jesus.

In the massive crowd that day was Doctor Dozous, who'd initially been highly sceptical of all the reports of apparitions down at the grotto. However, since the eyesight of his patient Louis Bouriette had been restored in a manner which completely defied science, he didn't know what to believe.

So the doctor pushed his way through all the onlookers until he was standing right next to Bernadette. At one point Bernadette's left hand moved directly over the large candle which she was holding in her right hand and remained there, with the flame burning between her fingers for fifteen minutes. The shocked crowd cried out on seeing this, but Bernadette seemed completely unaware of the commotion around her. When she'd come out of her ecstatic state the doctor examined her hand, which was completely unburned. Doctor Dozous was stunned by this phenomenon and so he asked someone to re-light the candle and he then pressed the flame up against Bernadette's left hand several times and she immediately cried out in pain each time.

Doctor Dozous became a staunch believer in Bernadette and the apparitions from what he witnessed that day, and after leaving Massabielle he went to the office of Commissioner Jacomet to formally record what he'd seen. This was his statement: "Bernadette seemed to be even more absorbed than usual in the Appearance upon which her gaze was riveted. I witnessed, as did also every one else there present, the fact which I am about to narrate. She was on her knees saying with fervent devotion the prayers of her Rosary which she held in her left hand while in her right was a large blessed candle, alight. The child was just beginning to make the usual ascent on her knees when suddenly she stopped and, her right hand joining her left, the flame of the big candle passed between the fingers of the latter. Though fanned by a fairly strong breeze, the flame produced no effect upon the skin which it was touching.

"Astonished at this strange fact, I forbade anyone there to interfere, and taking my watch in my hand, I studied the phenomenon attentively for a quarter of an hour. At the end of this time Bernadette, still in her ecstasy, advanced to the upper part of the Grotto, separating her hands. The flame thus ceased to touch her left hand. Bernadette finished her prayer and the splendour of the transfiguration left her face. She rose and was about to quit the Grotto when I asked her to show me her left hand. I examined it most carefully, but could not find the least trace of burning anywhere upon it.

"I then asked the person who was holding the candle to light it again and give it to me. I put it several times in succession under Bernadette's left hand but she drew it away quickly, saying, 'You are burning me!' I record this fact just as I have seen it without attempting to explain it. Many persons who were present at the time can confirm what I have said." Dr Dozous.

Three month interlude

8th April to 15th July 1858

There were now chaotic scenes at the grotto as thousands of people tried to get close to it, which prompted the authorities to barricade the site with boards to prevent access. However, the barricades were repeatedly destroyed by the crowds and they had to be painstakingly replaced by the police each time this happened.

At this time there was a fifteen year old boy named Henri Busquet living in the town of Nay, which was about 25 kilometres from Lourdes. Henri had been ill for about 15 months suffering from tuberculosis, and by the end of April 1858 his condition had worsened dramatically.

His chest was infected, he had a huge septic ulcer at the base of his neck, and the surrounding lymph glands were badly infected and inflamed. This was 70 years before Alexander Fleming discovered Penicillin in 1928 and so antibiotics didn't exist at the time. In desperation Henri asked to be taken to Lourdes, but his parents refused his request because he was so severely ill. However they pleaded with their neighbour to travel to Lourdes and to return with some water from the grotto.

On the night of 28th April, Henri was given the water and he immediately poured it on a dressing which he then placed over the huge ulcer as he and his family prayed together. Henri soon fell into a deep sleep, but when he awoke the next morning the tuberculosis had gone, the massive ulcer had completely scarred over, and the infected lymph glands had all returned to normal. Henri never suffered a relapse of this condition.

Professor Vergez declared without any hesitation: "This cure is beyond the laws of nature!"

On 4th May, Commissioner Jacomet instructed the police to remove all the candles from the grotto and he then made an announcement that the owners would have to collect them in person from the police station. But his efforts to draw attention away from the grotto failed miserably because the crowd collected their candles peacefully from the police station, lit them and then quietly walked together back to the grotto. The Police Commissioner had unwittingly caused the first public procession to the grotto in history! Jacomet later admitted, "Our opposition was in vain. Bernadette had the Immaculate Virgin Mary on her side!"

Baron Massy (Le Baron Oscar Massy) who was the prefect of the Hautes-Pyrenees and who was living in Tarbes, strongly denounced all the events that had been witnessed by thousands of people at the grotto, as well as Bernadette's own testimony of what she'd seen and heard there. So on 4th May he and Jacques Dutour, the Public Prosecutor went to Father Peyramale to inform him that they wanted to have Bernadette taken away and placed in the mental asylum in Tarbes.

But young Bernadette had now found support in Father Peyramale, who quickly came to her defence. He shouted, "I know my duty, as pastor of my parish and protector of my flock. Your own doctors find no abnormality in Bernadette. You will have to fell me to the ground, pass over my dead body, and trample it underfoot, before you touch a hair of the child's head."

Needless to say, their plan to incarcerate Bernadette in the mental asylum failed. But the area around the grotto remained barricaded and closed to the public, and the Soubirous family finally left the Cachot shortly after the seventeenth apparition.

Bernadette went on to make her First Holy Communion in the tiny chapel of the hospice in Lourdes run by the Sisters of Charity of Nevers on 3rd June, which appropriately is the Feast of Corpus Christi.

Bernadette later said, "My soul had been prepared for Jesus by his Mother, and my faith became enlightened in communion with my God."

Mademoiselle Estrade asked her, "What made you happier, Bernadette, First Holy Communion or the Apparitions?"

She answered, "The two go together. They cannot be compared. I only know I was very happy on both occasions."

Now Jean and Croisine Bouhort were one of the poorest families living in Lourdes at that time, and at the beginning of July they were experiencing a personal tragedy as their two year old son Justin, who was suffering from tuberculosis, was just about to die. Justin had been debilitated by fevers and had suffered convulsions since he was born and he'd never been able to walk at all in his short life.

Justin was now so ill that one of their neighbours had already made a shroud for him to be buried in after he passed away. The lady who'd made the shroud was trying to console Croisine and Jean as they stood around little Justin's cradle. When Justin's limbs went rigid and his eyes glassed over, and his breathing appeared to have stopped, his father said, "He's dead!"

But at these words, Croisine cried out, "He is not dead! The Holy Virgin of the grotto will cure him for me."

Jean, trying to contain his own sadness and console his wife, said to his neighbour, "She's mad with grief!"

But Croisine picked Justin up, wrapped him in her apron, and walked out the front door, with Jean and the neighbour pleading with her to stay in the house.

Croisine arrived at the grotto around 5 o'clock and there were still over 500 people there, saying their prayers or looking for something to take home with them from Massabielle as a souvenir. Ignoring the notice prohibiting entry to the grotto, she fell to her knees and prayed out loud before submerging Justin's naked body in the freezing water in the pit of the grotto that had recently been dug.

Some people in the crowd were shocked at the sight of Croisine doing this and shouted out, "The woman is mad!"

But Croisine shouted back, "Leave me alone! Leave me alone! I want to do what I can, and the good God and the Holy Virgin will do the rest."

By now the child was completely motionless and blue, so some people in the crowd called out, "The child's already dead. Let her do it; it's a poor mother whom sorrow has crazed."

Croisine held Justin under the water for at least 15 minutes as she prayed, and none of the abusive things people shouted at her would deter her from doing this. She eventually pulled Justin up out of the water, wrapped his still body in her apron, and carried him back home, praying to the Virgin Mary all the time as she walked.

When she entered the house, Jean looked down at Justin's lifeless body and said to her, "You see – he is dead."

But Croisine answered, "No, he's not dead. The Blessed Virgin will restore him to us!"

The mother placed Justin back in his cradle and leaned over to look at his face. Then she cried out aloud, "He breathes!"

Jean rushed over to the cradle and looked down in disbelief at Justin, who was indeed breathing again. Justin's eyes remained closed, but he was alive, and Croisine didn't sleep at all that night as she watched Justin's every breath.

Justin opened his eyes the following morning and he smiled at his mother, before she breast fed him. Later that day, Justin looked as though he wanted to get out of his cot, but Croisine was too scared to put him on the floor after all that he'd been through.

The following day, Croisine walked into the room and almost fainted. Justin, the infant who'd never walked in his life, had climbed out of his cot by himself and was walking around the room, going from one piece of furniture to the next. Justin ran over to his mum, who just burst into tears as she hugged him in disbelief.

When the neighbour who'd made the death shroud for Justin came across that day, she was completely stunned at the sight of the little boy walking around the house. She cried out, "It is he. It is really himself! Poor little Justin!"

Doctors Dozous, Vergez, and Peyrus, all conducted medical examinations of the boy and the medical report noted:

"The mother held her child for more than a quarter-of-an-hour, in the water of the fountain. She thus sought the cure of her child by proceedings absolutely condemned by experience and by medical reason, and yet she obtained it immediately…. The cure of the child took place without convalescence, in an entirely supernatural manner."

Eighteenth apparition

Friday 16th July 1858

By now, it had been over three months since Bernadette had last encountered The Virgin Mary, but on this Friday, the Feast of Our Lady of Mount Carmel, as she was kneeling in the parish church she once again felt an inner calling to go to Massabielle.

Bernadette and her Aunt Lucille were unable to get to the grotto itself because of the barriers that the police had erected, and Jacomet had also placed a large notice there which read, "Entrance to this property forbidden."

So Bernadette and Lucille walked over to join the huge crowd that had gathered on the far bank of the River Gave instead. Bernadette knelt on the ground, lit her candle and began to pray the Rosary and she immediately saw The Virgin Mary standing in the grotto, smiling at her. Bernadette said that despite the grotto being a few hundred metres away, the experience was just as intense as ever.

She wrote, "I thought I was at the Grotto, at the same distance as I was the other times. All I saw was Our Lady … She was more beautiful than ever."

At around 8pm the apparition disappeared. Bernadette later said:

"This would be the last time I would see her on this earth. I knew, because my Lady had prepared my soul for Jesus, and she would give me now to Him with whom I had communed. I knew, because of the way she held her head as she said goodbye. She left heaven in my heart and it has been there ever since."

- Chapter 3 -

A life changed forever

The eighteen apparitions of Our Lady to Bernadette between 11th February and 16th July 1858 would change her life forever, but it also presented a problem for the Catholic Church. It was undeniable that something supernatural had indeed happened at Massabielle, and the rationale for the massive crowds flocking there each day couldn't simply be put down to mass hysteria.

Many thousands of people, including dozens of public officials and doctors, had witnessed Bernadette's face being transfigured when she was in a state of ecstasy. On 25th February, a spring had miraculously appeared at the exact spot where Bernadette had scratched at the ground while in the presence of the apparition.

Then there were the instantaneous cures associated with touching the water from this spring, such as the healing of Louis Bouriette, who had instantly regained the sight in his right eye after bathing it in the water at the grotto. The paralysed fingers of Catherine Latapie-Chouat had been spontaneously healed after being immersed in the water from this spring on 1st March. There was also the remarkable case of the inexplicable healing of Croisine Bouhort's two year old son Justin after she'd submerged him in the water for at least 15 minutes. These and several other healings had been investigated by leading physicians, who simply couldn't explain them in terms of medicine or science.

The shattering revelation by Bernadette that the lady had said that she was The Immaculate Conception clearly had implications for the Church. If Bernadette was telling the truth and The Virgin Mary really had appeared to her at the grotto 18 times, then it was clearly incumbent on the Church to act upon the revelations that Bernadette had been given. The two most obvious of these were a call to repentance, and her instruction that a chapel should be built which the people should go to in procession.

By now, some senior members of the Church hierarchy had met with Bernadette and had asked her questions about her experiences at the grotto. One of these was Charles-Thomas Thibault who was the Bishop of Montpellier, and another was Paul-Armand Cardon de

Garsignies who was the Bishop of Soissons. Both men were left with a feeling that in Bernadette they were dealing with a sincere, straight talking, honest young woman.

As Lourdes fell under the jurisdiction of Monsignor Bertrand-Severe Mascarou Laurence of Tarbes, Bishops Cardon de Garsignies and Thibault asked him if he would launch a full investigation. Monsignor Laurence agreed to this and set up a Commission to thoroughly investigate all the events at Massabielle, with the enquiry starting as early as the 28th of July 1858.

He wrote: "To deny the possibility of supernatural happenings would be to plod along in the rut worn by the scepticism of the last century."

The bishop used three criteria to establish the authenticity of the Apparitions. The first was the reliability of Bernadette herself. The second were the 'spiritual fruits' that were associated with the Apparitions. The third criterion was the outcome of the investigation into all the claims of miraculous cures.

Exhaustive interviews were then conducted with a huge number of people who'd stood just metres from Bernadette at the grotto. Anselme Lacade, the Mayor of Lourdes, whose family owned the Lacade Mill, even requested that a sample of the water from the spring be chemically analysed. So samples were sent to a chemistry professor in Toulouse for analysis, but the tests showed that there was nothing unusual about the chemical composition of the water.

The Commission wouldn't conclude all its meticulous investigations into the events at Massabielle for three long years!

Father Arder, who was Bernadette's parish priest for a brief time at Bartres, had always been impressed by her. He was also a staunch believer in the earlier apparitions of the Virgin Mary to Maximin Giraud and Melanie Calvat at La Salette-Fallavaux in 1846.

He said this about Bernadette: "She seems to me like a flower surrounded in divine perfume. I assure you that on many occasions, when I have seen her, I have thought of the children of La Salette. Certainly, if the Blessed Virgin appeared to Maximino and Melania, she did so in order for them to become as simple and pious as she is."

On another occasion Father Arder said, "Look at this small child. When the Blessed Virgin wants to appear on earth she chooses children like her."

It was in July 1858 that Father Peyramale personally stepped in to help the Soubirous family by paying the rent of the Lacade Mill for them. This must have been an immense relief for Francois after the long years of financial worries and the ever present danger of facing eviction.

In an attempt to ease the growing frustration caused by the ban on people visiting the grotto, the Emperor of France finally ordered that the barricades be removed on 5th October 1858. This was the same man who'd previously shown great hostility to the Catholic Church, putting restrictions on Catholic newspapers and even on the charitable Saint Vincent de Paul Society. The faithful felt a huge sense of relief and the grotto at Massabielle immediately became a peaceful site of pilgrimage once again, with candles burning throughout the night.

By now, dozens of people had claimed that they'd been miraculously healed after drinking the water from the spring, or applying it to their bodies, and one such healing involved 57 year old Madeleine Rizan, who lived in the town of Nay.

Madeleine had contracted Cholera in 1832 and the infection had left her paralysed on the left side of her body. She'd been bed-ridden for the last 20 years, from 1838 onwards, and she was in terrible pain from bed sores and other health conditions. Madeleine was so ill that she received Extreme Unction (Sacrament of the Sick) in September 1858 and by 16th October she'd deteriorated so much that her death was now imminent.

In desperation her daughter obtained some water from the grotto in Lourdes and gave it to her mother to sip and to put on her body. Incredibly, Madeleine quickly recovered, but not to her bed-ridden state of semi paralysis! Her paralysis left her completely, her sores disappeared and she was even able to walk, dress and eat on her own from that day onwards. In fact, Madeleine lived a normal life until her death 11 years later in 1869.

News of Madeleine's healing reached the Moreau family living in Tartas, about 130 kilometres from Lourdes. Sixteen year old Marie

Moreau had contracted an inflammatory infection of the eyes in early 1858 which had left her so visually impaired that she was virtually blind. Marie's father was so desperate that he travelled all the way to Lourdes to get some water from the grotto for his daughter.

Then on Monday 8th November 1858, the Moreau family began a Novena of prayers and that night Marie soaked a bandage in the water, tied it over her eyes and went to bed. The next morning when she removed the bandage, her vision had returned to normal. Marie's healing was so complete that she was even able to resume her studies at Bordeaux.

Now as part of the Commission's investigation, Bernadette was formally questioned yet again on 17th November 1858, but despite the rigour of the questioning, 14 year old Bernadette remained calm and composed throughout.

Then in 1859, the esteemed Professor Henri Vergez, who was at the Faculty of Medicine at Montpellier, was appointed as the medical consultant to the Episcopal Commission which was investigating all the inexplicable cures at Lourdes. After exhaustive research, interviews and medical examinations, Doctor Vergez and his team of doctors concluded that it was impossible to explain seven of the healings from a medical viewpoint.

He said, "In glancing at these cures, taken collectively, one is at once struck by the ease and spontaneity with which they spring from their producing cause. In them we seem to be in the presence of an open violation and complete upsetting of therapeutic methods, of a declared contradiction of scientific precepts …… Such phenomena are beyond the comprehension of the human mind."

Doctor Vergez also said, "Here we have certainly to deal with a contingent force superior to the forces of nature, and consequently extraneous to the water which this force makes use of …"

Doctors Vergez and Dozou had become involved in the events at Lourdes as medical professionals, who would denounce any claims of supernatural healing without overwhelming scientific evidence. But on seeing this shattering evidence before their eyes, they'd both moved from being sceptics to firm believers in the miraculous nature of these events.

There was another addition to the Soubirous family when Louise gave birth to a baby boy on 10th September 1859, who they named Pierre-Bernard.

Bernadette had to contend with a large number of visitors who wanted to ask her questions about the Apparitions, and some of them got a little too personal. One person asked, "Why don't you drink from the water of the fountain? This water has cured others, why not you?"

But Bernadette simply replied, "The Blessed Virgin perhaps desires for me to suffer. I need it."

Not satisfied with her reply, the person asked, "Why you more than others?"

And to this question, Bernadette just answered, "The good God knows."

Another person challenged Bernadette on whether she'd been assured of going to heaven, by saying, "The Virgin said you will be happy in another world; therefore are you sure you are going to heaven?"

But Bernadette responded, "Oh no, this is only if I do what is good."

In was in July 1860 that Father Peyramale asked the Sisters of Charity of Nevers, who cared for the sick in the hospice in Lourdes, and who also taught in the school there, if they would allow Bernadette to live in the hospice. He was concerned about the effects that all the publicity and a never ending stream of visitors who were coming to see Bernadette were having on her health.

So from July 1860, Bernadette found a home with the Sisters of Charity of Nevers in the Lourdes hospice, but she was cautioned not to attract attention to herself from people outside the hospice while she was under their care. Louise cried the day that Bernadette left home, but she knew in her heart that her daughter would be better protected in the hospice. So the 16 year old Bernadette was taken on as an 'au pair boarder' although she sometimes went home to spend the night with her family at the Lacade Mill.

At the hospice school, Sister Elizabeth was given responsibility for teaching Bernadette and so she slowly learned how to read and write, to speak French and to sew and embroider.

When Bernadette first entered the hospice, the Mother Superior said to Sister Elizabeth, "It is said she is not too intelligent. See if there is a possibility to do something with her."

But after just a short time spent teaching Bernadette, Sister Elizabeth went to see the Mother Superior and said, "My dear Mother, you have been misled. Bernadette is very intelligent and retains very well the doctrine given!"

On another occasion, Sister Elizabeth said, "I found in her a vivid intelligence, perfect innocence and an exquisite heart."

In many ways, Bernadette was like a typical teenage girl, playful and fun loving, and occasionally mischievous with it. She once shocked the Sister who was giving a very boring French lesson by secretly passing around snuff, which resulted in all the kids having a fit of sneezing.

Another Sister wasn't very impressed when she saw Bernadette throwing her shoe out of the classroom window and asking a girl named Julie Garros to fill it with strawberries for her.

Bernadette went through a brief phase of being a little vain, wanting to look good, just as most young people do, but Sister Victorina observed, "The fever passed rapidly and didn't harm her profound piety."

Bernadette loved being around the youngsters and so she was often asked to look after the younger children in the hospice school. One of them said, "Bernadette was very simple. When we asked her to take care of us, she did so in such a way that she seemed like another child playing with us, not letting us be reminded of her miraculous adventure. Raised with the thought that our friend saw the Virgin Mary, we consider her very natural as a child of today who has seen the president of the Republic."

It was a wise decision of Father Peyramale to place Bernadette under the protection of the Sisters, as it meant that it was now more difficult for large numbers of people to question her each and every day. It also put up a barrier to prevent various officials from hassling young Bernadette. However, even in the hospice Bernadette was called in for questioning several times a day, and sometimes it became too much for her and she would begin to cry. Sometimes Sister Victorina would comfort her by saying, "Courage! The Apparitions were for others as well as for yourself."

In the hospice, Bernadette saw Christian love in action right before her eyes, as she watched the sisters care for the sick, the elderly and the destitute, as well as educating many young girls from deprived families.

She said, "I love the poor. I love taking care of the sick. I will stay with the Sisters of Charity of Nevers."

The Episcopal Commission that had been set up by Monsignor Laurence finally ended after three and a half years when the bishop himself announced the result of its findings in a pastoral letter he wrote on **18ᵗʰ January 1862**.

"The testimony of the young girl presents all the guarantees we can desire. First of all, her sincerity cannot be called into question. Who, when he meets with her, can do aught but admire the simplicity, the candour, the modesty of this child? While all around her talk about the marvels revealed to her, she alone keeps silent; she speaks only when questioned and then she relates everything without affectation and with a touching simplicity; and to the numerous questions she is plied with, she answers, without hesitation, clearly, precisely, aptly, in words stamped with a strong conviction … She is always in agreement with her own statements, she has always maintained what she has said without adding or suppressing any fact during the different interrogations to which she has been subjected …

"But if Bernadette has not wished to deceive, could she not have been the subject of self-deception? Has she not believed that she has seen and listened to what she has neither perceived nor heard? Has she not been the subject of hallucinations? – How could we believe such a thing of her? The wisdom of her replies testifies to the upright character of this child, her unruffled imagination, a good sense surpassing her age. Religious sentiments have never presented in her an over-excited disposition. We have never established in the nature of this young girl any intellectual disorder or impaired judgment, or singularity of character, nor morbid affection, which could predispose her to imaginary creations …

"We judge that Mary Immaculate, Mother of God, really appeared to Bernadette on the 11ᵗʰ February, 1858 and on the following days to the number of 18 days in all in the Grotto of Massabielle, near the town of Lourdes, that this apparition is endowed with all the characters of truth and that the faithful are justified in believing it with certainty."

Bishop Laurence also declared that seven of the cures that had been investigated by Professor Henri Vergez and his team were indeed 'miraculous.'

What would have been music to Bernadette's ears was that he also announced: "We propose to build a chapel by the grotto which is now the property of the Diocese of Tarbes."

Now the building of new churches in France was strictly regulated, and according to the Concordat of 1801 it was necessary to have Imperial authorisation before construction of a church could begin. However, Monsignor Laurence threw himself into this new endeavour with great enthusiasm and had already been granted Imperial approval before his announcement of 18th January 1862! In fact by this time he'd already been discussing his plans for a chapel with Hippolyte Louis Durand, who specialised in the design of medieval style churches.

There was a well known French journalist and author named Louis Veuillot who wrote a detailed account of all the apparitions for a newspaper called l'Univers. When the article was published it created a great deal of controversy, but when Bernadette was asked what she thought of the article she humbly replied, "I hardly know how to read."

Bernadette was eventually fatigued by her duties and the constant questioning, and in April 1862 she fell ill and collapsed in the hospice. A doctor who worked there was called over to examine Bernadette and he prescribed some medication to help her recover, but she secretly asked for some water from the grotto to be brought to her instead.

Bernadette said, "A moment after sipping it, I felt as though a mountain were lifted off my chest."

The doctor was really shocked at the speed of her recovery and said proudly, "My medicine worked well!"

But Bernadette looked at the doctor and replied, "I did not take it."

To which the proud physician responded, "Well, you weren't as sick as you thought you were!"

Baron Massy, the prefect of the Hautes-Pyrenees, who'd initially been so derisory of Bernadette's claims, passed away on 10th August 1862. Referring to all the officials who made life so difficult for her and her family, Bernadette said that they had all finally believed in the

Apparitions and that they'd all died with the crucifix pressed to their lips.

Back in Lourdes, construction of the chapel above the grotto began when the first foundation stone was laid on 14th October 1862, and it was fitting that Bernadette's father, Francois worked as a labourer on the crypt for several months.

After the Apparitions had ended at Massabielle, someone had placed a small plaster statue of the Virgin Mary at the grotto. But in September 1863 it was decided that a sculptor should be commissioned to produce a new statue of the Blessed Virgin, one that closely reflected the way she'd been dressed and her demeanor during the Apparitions.

The de Lacour Sisters offered to pay for the work to be done and a sculptor named Joseph-Hugues Fabisch from Lyons was given the commission and asked to carve the statue from Carrara marble. Fabisch then travelled down to Lourdes on 17th September 1863 to get a detailed description from Bernadette on exactly how the Virgin Mary had looked when she had appeared to her.

Fabisch began working on a model and after two months he had a photograph of it taken, which he then sent to Bernadette in the hospice. Bernadette discussed the photograph of the statue with Father Peyramale, who wrote down her constructive criticism of the model, and he then communicated her comments back to the sculptor in Lyon.

At this time, the hospice and school in Lourdes fell under the jurisdiction of Bishop Forcade of Nevers, and so he occasionally visited the Mother Superior and the sisters who were working there. But when the bishop paid the hospice a visit on 27th September 1863, he walked straight into the kitchen looking for Bernadette, and he found her sitting on a wooden block scraping carrots for the sister's dinner. The bishop then made some small talk with Bernadette before gently asking her if she was inclined to get married one day, to which she responded, "Oh, that is not for me!"

So Bishop Forcade then asked if she'd ever contemplated joining the Convent of the Sisters of Charity of Nevers. Bernadette, in her typical self-effacing manner, replied that she didn't know anything, that she wasn't good at anything and that she was too poor to be able to join the convent. Bernadette was also concerned that her frail health might be an obstacle to her in the carrying out of her duties.

However the bishop reassured her that if it was evident that she had a vocation, then exceptions to the normal conditions of entry could be made. He suggested that Bernadette should take some time to think it over and that if she decided that she had a calling, then he would take care of everything else.

Bernadette's mother, Louise, gave birth to a baby boy on 4th February 1864 and she named him Jean, in memory of her other son who'd only survived for two months.

The sculptor Fabisch completed his statue by the end of March 1864 and promptly brought it through to Lourdes several days before the date set for its dedication. Although most people were delighted with his work, Bernadette studied it carefully and then said, "No, it is not she!"

Bernadette later said that the sculptor had made Our Lady look too big and that the statue didn't capture her smile correctly, but she also said that it wasn't his fault because no marble could possibly capture her 'living sacredness.' She wrote, "He was not to blame. In Heaven he will understand."

Poor Fabisch would later admit that Bernadette's reaction to his work was the greatest sorrow of his artistic life. Nevertheless, he carried his statue himself in a formal procession to the grotto on 4th April 1864. It would be this same statue that would greet many millions of pilgrims to Lourdes over the years. Bernadette and Father Peyramale had planned on joining the procession, but by coincidence they were both taken ill on that day and were unable to make it.

It was in August 1864 that Bernadette approached Sister Alexandrine Roques, the Mother Superior of the hospice, saying, "My dear Mother, I have prayed much to know if I'm called to religious life. I believe the answer is 'yes.' I would like to enter the congregation if I'm accepted. Permit me to write to the Bishop."

The Mother Superior was overcome with emotion and began to cry with joy at the news, and she hugged Bernadette close to her. However, between the time of Bernadette writing to the Bishop of Nevers, and her receiving confirmation that she'd been accepted, her baby brother Jean passed away on 11th September at the age of just seven months.

Bernadette's request to join the Sisters of Charity of Nevers was initially viewed with some scepticism by Mother Josefina Imbert, the Mother Superior of the convent, who was concerned about the effect that it would have if the famous visionary came to join them.

However, Bernadette received confirmation that she'd been accepted on 19th November 1864, but she unfortunately fell ill once again, which delayed her induction into the convent by over 19 months.

Incredibly, the Soubirous family would then suffer yet another tragedy when Justin died on 1st February 1865, just a few weeks before his tenth birthday. Bernadette unfortunately had no choice but to stay on at the hospice in Lourdes as she struggled with her grief and poor health. Tragically, she had by now lost four of her brothers.

The depths of Bernadette's faith when faced with personal tragedy are clear by what she said about her brother: "Justin never saw his tenth birthday. He was the fourth child my parents had seen die. That made four of our family in Heaven to keep our places ready till we meet again in the Communion of Saints."

A railway connection to Lourdes was eventually completed in 1866 and a railway station (gare de Lourdes) was opened on 20th April of that year. This was excellent timing because the chapel above the grotto was completed in May 1866, with the crypt being blessed on 19th May. This was Pentecost Sunday, and Bernadette and her family were all at the blessing ceremony on that special day.

Louise gave birth for the last time in 1866, but because the baby girl, who they also named Louise, died within a few minutes of birth, the birth and death of this baby were not registered anywhere.

By the time the crypt had been blessed, the Bishop of Nevers had given responsibility for maintaining and protecting the shrine to the Garaison Fathers. This was a good decision, because with the new railway connection in place, it didn't take long before the faithful were pouring into Lourdes by train from Tarbes.

But even before the chapel had opened to the public it had become obvious that a much bigger church would have to be built to accommodate the large numbers of pilgrims that were now visiting

Lourdes. So the architect Hippolyte Louis Durrand was asked to draw up plans for the Basilica of the Immaculate Conception, and construction of this Gothic style church began in 1866. The basilica would be built above the existing chapel, which would then become the crypt of the new basilica, and it would be large enough to accommodate 550 people.

On 3rd July 1866, Bernadette went to the grotto for the very last time. By then Bernadette's health had recovered enough for her to be able to take up her calling and to join the Sisters of Charity of Nevers. Bernadette now had no doubt that this was how she wanted to spend the rest of her life, and she'd earlier written, "I'm more convinced than ever to leave the world. Now I have definitely decided and hope to leave it soon."

When Bernadette went to visit Massabielle for the last time on 3rd July 1866, she was accompanied by a few nuns, and on reaching the grotto she fell to the ground, kissed it and began to cry. After some time the nuns tried to persuade her to leave, but she kept asking if she could remain there a bit longer, and in the end they had to use a little physical persuasion to pry her away from the grotto. As Bernadette was being led away, she turned around to look at the rock one final time. One of the nuns, seeing Bernadette's genuine outpouring of sadness, said to her, "You know the Blessed Virgin will hear you wherever you are."

She replied, "Yes, but the Grotto was my Heaven on earth."

Bernadette and her family gathered for their last meal together in the Lacade Mill that same evening. The 22 year old Bernadette said farewell to her family the next day, Wednesday 4th July, but before leaving she said a beautiful prayer. It mirrored the wonderful prayer of the Virgin Mary, known as the Magnificat, which Mary said when she was carrying Jesus in her womb, as she entered the house of her relative Elizabeth, in Judea.

Bernadette said, "Yes, dear Mother, you have come down to the earth to appear to a weak child. You, Queen of heaven and earth, have chosen what was the most humble according to the world."

The convent used by the Sisters of Charity in Nevers is named the Convent of Saint Gildard, and Bernadette arrived there by train on the evening of Saturday 7th July. It was the first and last time that she ever travelled by train in her life. At that time, Superiors didn't come through to greet the postulants who arrived at night and so Bernadette and the others just wandered through the corridors in the dark to their dormitory and quietly went to bed.

That night the reality of her new situation must have sunk in because Bernadette cried in her bed just like all the other postulants. She also cried for most of the following day, despite being consoled by the sisters and told that her tears were a sign of a true vocation.

The Mother Superior was Mother Josefina Imbert, who initially had reservations about Bernadette coming to the convent, and the Mistress of Novices was 40 year old Mother Marie-Therese Vauzou. It would appear that neither of these women made life at all easy for the young Bernadette.

On Sunday 8th July, her first full day at the convent, all 300 Sisters were gathered together and Bernadette, still wearing her clothes from home, was given the daunting task of speaking to them all about the Apparitions. Before beginning, she was told that it would be the first and the last time that she would speak about the subject!

In the convent, Bernadette remained homesick and her tuberculosis flared up at the beginning of August, making her so seriously ill that she was taken to the infirmary. One night in October 1866, her bouts of coughing and asthma attacks were so severe that Doctor Robert Saint-Cyr was convinced that she wouldn't survive the night.

So Mother Marie-Therese sent for Bishop Forcade, who quickly came to the infirmary to administer the Last Rites. In the end he was unable to give her the Eucharist (the Viaticum) because of her coughing fits and the blood that she was vomiting up.

The Mother Superior also thought that Bernadette was going to die and so she discussed with Bishop Forcade the possibility of allowing her to take her vows on her death bed before she passed away. The Bishop agreed to this and so he went to the infirmary to conduct the ceremony, where he first explained to Bernadette that she was going to die, before beginning the Rite.

As Bernadette was too ill to speak, she had to give her consent to the questions by hand gestures. At the end of the ceremony she was given the profession veil and she took the name Sister Marie-Bernard, which was her baptismal name.

Bernadette later fell asleep, with everyone expecting her not to survive the night, and yet she awoke the next morning feeling somewhat better. She said to the Mother Superior, "My Reverend Mother, you allowed me to do my religious profession, thinking I was going to die. Well look, I'm not going to die!"

The Mother Superior felt that she'd somehow been duped and told Bernadette that she was a foolish girl for having led everyone to believe that she was about to die. Mother Imbert also threatened to take away her veil and return her to the Novitiate if she hadn't died by the following morning. Bernadette, humble and accepting as ever, simply responded, "As you wish, Reverend Mother."

So Bernadette survived this terrible bout of tuberculosis and began to recuperate in the infirmary. Bernadette later returned to the Novitiate, but she soon received the terrible news that her mother Louise had passed away. Louise had died peacefully on 8th December 1866 at the age of just 41.

In her grief, Bernadette prayed, "My God, You have willed this! I accept the chalice you have given me. May Your Name be blessed."

Her complete acceptance of God's will at times of loss and during periods of life-threatening illness shows just how deep her faith was. Bernadette would later say that her mother's death had convinced her that 'life is only Heaven's waiting-room.'

The other novices could see that Bernadette's sickness was a constant affliction to her, and yet her temperament remained friendly and happy throughout. They also noticed that she was treated more harshly than the rest of them and they would sometimes remark, "It is not good to be Bernadette!"

Why this was the case is unclear. Bernadette was so humble and unassuming that it was very easy for others to underestimate her, and perhaps her superiors wanted to show everyone else in the convent that she wasn't going to get any favours because of who she was.

An example of just how humble she was can be seen in the reaction of one of the postulants on seeing Bernadette for the very first time in

1867. The postulant, Antoinette Dalias, said to one of the Sisters, "I've been in Nevers for three days, and no one has shown me Bernadette."

The Sister replied, "That's Bernadette beside you."

Antoinette looked over at Bernadette and said, "Not that?"

Bernadette came forward, gently took the postulant's hand and said, "Yes, Mademoiselle, just that."

Bernadette's prayers were unstructured and said from the heart, which was different to the regimented way of praying that was prevalent all around her. She simply prayed as a person would speak to someone who was standing right next to them. But Bernadette prayed the Rosary often, just as she'd been brought up to do since she was a little child. She carried her Rosary around with her, and at times of difficulty she would immediately take it out and begin praying.

On 20th August 1867, Monsignor Laurence made a wonderful act of kindness by purchasing the Lacade Mill and then giving it to the Soubirous family to rescue them from poverty.

Two months later, Bernadette was one of 44 novices who made her Religious Profession on 30th October 1867. By now she was 23 years of age and she again took the name Sister Marie-Bernard. A short while later, the Mother Superior allocated duties to each of the newly professed sisters but she couldn't think of a role for Bernadette. When the bishop asked Mother Imbert what role she was to be given, she replied that Bernadette was a little stupid and that she was good for nothing!

The bishop then looked down at Bernadette who was kneeling in front of him and said to her, "I give you the assignment of praying."

In the end Bernadette was allocated the lowliest of jobs, which was working as a cleaner and assistant in the infirmary, and although it must have been humiliating for her, she took on her role with enthusiasm. Her title was 'Assistant Community Infirmarian.'

She later said, "When one is espoused to Jesus Christ, one should say yes in physical and emotional pain, without any ifs or buts."

Bernadette would only speak to the Sisters or her superiors about the Apparitions when questioned, as she'd been asked to do, but a large number of people visited her at St Gildard, curious to find out what the Blessed Virgin had said to her, or to petition her to pray for some or other intention.

Bernadette always loved being around children and one day a little four year old said to her, "You have seen the Blessed Virgin, Sister. Was she beautiful?"

Bernadette replied, "So beautiful, that once you have seen Her, you would willingly die to see Her again."

However she still had to put up with the hostility of all the sceptics, although by now she was well used to it. One person challenged Bernadette on what she said the Virgin Mary had been wearing during the Apparitions, saying that Our Lady could never have worn a blue coloured sash because it was not a liturgical colour.

Unfazed by this, Bernadette just replied, "I don't know anything about liturgy, but I do know the Lady's sash was blue."

But when Bernadette didn't have visitors she just lived a life of obscurity, performing her menial tasks as well as she could and as well as her poor health allowed.

Bishop Laurence, the man who'd convened the Episcopal Commission to investigate the events at Massabielle in 1858, and who'd seen through the construction of the chapel above the grotto, passed away on 30th January 1870.

Bernadette's father, Francois, died the following year at the Lacade Mill in Lourdes on Saturday 4th March 1871. After hearing the news, she walked over to a statue of the Virgin Mary and began to pray, crying as she did so, which attracted the attention of one of the Sisters.

The Sister came over to try and console her, but before the Sister could say a word, Bernadette said, "My Sister, always have great devotion to the agony of our Saviour. Saturday in the afternoon I prayed to Jesus in agony for all those who would die at this moment, and it was precisely the moment my father entered eternity. What a consolation it is for me to have helped him."

She also said this about her father: "He died as he lived, in deep faith, and with a quiet longing to be with God."

In the Convent, Bernadette still had to endure the harsh treatment of her superiors and the ongoing scepticism of some of the Sisters, but she rationalised her situation by remembering the words of Jesus.

Bernadette once said, "When my emotions are too strong, I remember the words of Our Lord: 'It is I, don't be afraid.' I immediately appreciate and thank Our Lord for this grace of rejections and humiliations from my Superiors and sisters. It is the love of this Good Master who would remove the roots from this tree of pride. The more little I become, the more I grow in the Heart of Jesus."

Unfortunately Bernadette lost the rosary that her sister Toinette had given to her in 1856, which was the one that she'd prayed with during the Apparitions. Regarding the making of this devotion she said, "The Rosary became my way of prayer, indeed my way of life. To hold it in ones hands brought serenity and peace."

Construction of the Basilica of the Immaculate Conception, with its 70 metre high spire, was completed in 1871, and the basilica was blessed on 15th August of that year. In 1871 about 28,000 pilgrims arrived in Lourdes by train, and in 1872 the number of pilgrims had soared to 140,000.

Bernadette continued working at the infirmary in Nevers, but in the Autumn of 1873 she was again hospitalised due to her bronchial problems. It was then decided that she was too ill to continue her role as an assistant in the Infirmary, and so Bernadette was asked to take on the role of Assistant Sacristan at the beginning of 1874.

Bernadette loved this role because it allowed her to spend far more time in the chapel, in the presence of the Blessed Sacrament, and here she was only lightly supervised and so she was able to devote far more time to prayer. Her role involved setting out the liturgical books for the readings at Mass, controlling the priest's vestments, ensuring there was wine and a sufficient number of hosts for Communion, cleaning the chapel, chalices, ciboria, altar linen, hand towels, etc.

Although Bernadette was only 30 years of age, she was now suffering from chronic asthma and chest pains, tuberculosis, abscesses, bone decay and a tumour on her knee.

On 8th September 1877, Father Peyramale, the initial sceptic turned staunch witness to the Apparitions, died in Lourdes.

For over 1500 years, the 8th of September had been celebrated as the birthday of the Virgin Mary, and Bernadette was quick to recognise the significance of Father Peyramale dying on that very day.

She said, "He began the processions I could never organise, he built the chapel I could never build. Our Lady had requested but a chapel. He gave her a basilica. Surely, when he died on her birthday, she gave him Heaven."

When Bernadette looked back on the lives of Father Peyramale and her own father, she said that their deaths showed that it was madness to become too deeply attached to anything on earth, because we soon have to leave it all behind for heaven.

Bernadette was by now seriously ill and it was in September 1877 that she said to the Sisters, "I will not last long now."

Sometimes people would ask her why she didn't take some of the water from Lourdes to heal herself and on one occasion she answered, "It's no use. Our Lady told me I would die young."

Bernadette professed her eternal vows on 22nd September 1878 during a short period when she was feeling better, but on 11th December she was placed in the Infirmary once again, and this time she would never leave it. The Infirmary where Bernadette had spent so much time in the care of others had now become her home.

She said, "My bed became my little white chapel. Then it became my cross. Eventually it became a crucifix, when I could only lie on it and suffer."

Bernadette developed terrible bedsores all over her back and the ulcers in her leg caused by the tuberculosis burst. She also developed abscesses in her ears which made her deaf for a time. However, it was clear to the Sisters around her that she'd accepted whatever suffering was sent her way.

Bernadette said that she'd decided that her weapons would be prayer and sacrifice, which she would hold onto until her last breath. Then the weapon of sacrifice would fall from her hand, but the weapon of prayer would follow her to Heaven.

The last few months of Bernadette's life were very difficult for her and she experienced the 'Dark night of the Soul' where she lost her inner peace, felt despair and doubted whether she was worthy of going to heaven.

The term 'Dark night of the Soul' has been used since Saint John of the Cross, the Spanish 16th century priest and mystic, wrote Ascent of Mount Carmel and the Dark Night. Saint John believed in 'purgative contemplation', where God deliberately darkens a person's will, intellect and senses in order to test their love for Him. The objective of this isn't to harm the person in any way, but rather to refine and perfect their faith so that they can become ever more united to His love.

Saint Therese of Lisieux also experienced this, and her darkness was over doubts about the existence of eternity, and she said to her fellow Carmelite nuns, "If you only knew what darkness I am plunged into." However, Therese emerged from this period of darkness with a deeper faith than she had before.

Mother Teresa of Calcutta also experienced this spiritual doubt, abandonment and feelings of being unworthy for many years, and she only had brief respites without this darkness in her life.

Jesus himself suffered mental anguish in the Garden of Gethsemane and later on the cross when he cried out, "Eloi, Eloi lama sabachthani" ("My God, my God, Why have you forsaken me?")

During this difficult period for Bernadette, one of the Sisters told her that she was going to pray to God to console her, but Bernadette asked her not to pray for that, but rather to pray that she would be granted strength and patience.

On Easter Monday, Bernadette took the hand of her close friend Sister Bernard Dalias, and said, "Goodbye, Bernard, this time it is the last." Sister Dalias was Antoinette Dalias, who as a postulant 12 years earlier had said, "Not that" on meeting Bernadette for the very first time, and since that day the two had become very close friends.

On Wednesday 16th April 1879, Bernadette asked one of the Sisters if she would tie her crucifix to her hand just in case she became too weak to hold it any more. She then looked over at a statue of the Virgin Mary and said, "I have seen her. How beautiful she is, and how I long to go to her."

She asked Sister Nathalie Portat to pray with her, and while holding the crucifix Bernadette said, "My God I love You, with all my heart, with all my soul, with all my strength."

Sister Nathalie and Bernadette began to say a Hail Mary and then Bernadette said, "I am thirsty." She made the Sign of the Cross and after sipping a little water, she quietly passed away at 3:15 in the afternoon.

Sister Bernard Dalias said, "As soon as she was dead, Bernadette's face became young and peaceful again, with a look of purity and blessedness."

Some of the Sisters in the Infirmary then clothed Bernadette's body in her religious habit and it was while doing this that they noticed something unusual - Bernadette's body was still supple. Sister de Vigouroux said, "We had no difficulty in doing so for her body was supple even though she had been dead for two hours."

Throughout that evening, all the nuns paid their respects by visiting Bernadette and saying a little prayer beside her. At around 11 o'clock in the morning, her body was placed in a temporary coffin and then taken down to Saint Joseph's Chapel, the little Gothic chapel in the convent garden. The coffin was draped in white linen and lilies, and a crown of little white roses was placed over her black veil.

The Sisters put a crucifix and the formula of her Perpetual Vows between her clasped hands and entwined Bernadette's Rosary beads around them. Her body lay in the open coffin for two days, during which time thousands of people journeyed to Nevers in the pouring rain to see her.

Four of the Sisters stood around her coffin as people passed slowly by, and these nuns were handed all sorts of objects that people wanted to be blessed, such as rosaries, medals, crucifixes and even labourer's tools! The nuns quietly took them and then touched the objects against Bernadette's hands, before returning them.

Bernadette's Requiem Mass had originally been arranged for Friday 18th but due to the huge number of people wanting to see her, it went ahead the next day, which was a beautiful Saturday morning. The Mass, celebrated by Canon Greuzard, began at 10 o'clock with Bishop Lelong and Father Remi Sempe present, as well as Father Pomian,

Bernadette's former confessor. Unfortunately none of Bernadette's relations were able to make it, but the Requiem Mass was packed with all the nuns, and about 80 priests were also present. Bishop Lelong said that the work of God had been evident in the humble, virginal life of Bernadette, and in the marvels of Lourdes which were the consequence of her faithful witness.

Her open casket, which was made of lead encased in oak, was carried to Saint Joseph's chapel and a huge crowd filled the courtyards, the terrace and the garden. After the Absolution, the congregation all sang, 'Salve Regina.' At about 2 pm Bernadette's coffin was sealed, during which time the massive crowd outside the chapel recited the Rosary, with Father Sempe announcing one of the Glorious Mysteries before the start of each decade. Finally, on 22nd May 1879, which was Ascension Day, Bernadette's coffin was placed in a specially built vault inside St Joseph's chapel.

Monsignor Benoit-Marie Langenieux had been appointed the Bishop of Tarbes in 1873, but he held this office for less than a year. However in his short time at Tarbes he conceived the idea of building a much larger church than the Basilica of the Immaculate Conception, to accommodate the ever growing number of pilgrims visiting Lourdes. So he contracted the architect Leopold Hardy to design the Basilica of Our Lady of the Rosary of Lourdes, which would be situated below and in front of the existing basilica, and it would be large enough to accommodate 1500 worshippers. The foundation digging for this Byzantine style basilica began in 1883.

It was also in 1883 that Father Remi Sempe of the Garaison Fathers, who was the first rector of the sanctuary at Lourdes, decided that there needed to be a facility in the town to investigate the large number of cases of miraculous healings. So he asked Doctor Georges-Fernand Dunot de Saint-Maclou to set up such a facility, and the result was the formation of the Bureau des Constatations Medicales in 1883. The Doctor became its first president, and he assembled a team of physicians to rigorously examine all the cases where people believed that they'd been miraculously cured after having visited the grotto.

Bishop Langenieux's dream of building a church in honour of Our Lady was realised when the Basilica of Our Lady of the Rosary was consecrated in 1901, and fortunately he was still alive to see it!

- Chapter 4 -

The long road to sainthood

Letters from people claiming to have been miraculously healed after drinking or touching the water at the grotto, or after having prayed for Bernadette's intercession, soon started to arrive at St Gildard's Convent. So in Rome in February 1907, Cardinal Vives asked Bishop Francois-Leon Gauthey of Nevers to gather information on Bernadette to decide if there was a case for her beatification.

The following year on 20th August 1908, in St Joseph's Chapel at the Convent of Saint Gildard, Bishop Gauthey constituted the Ecclesiastical Court which would conduct the first enquiry into Bernadette's life.

The initial enquiry is known as the 'Informative Process' and it gathers information on a person's virtues, their reputation for sanctity and the miracles associated with them. Ultimately a total of 132 sessions of the Court were convened, and evidence was taken from priests, nuns, lay people and also the surviving members of Bernadette's own family.

Before closing the Ecclesiastical Court, Bishop Gauthey ordered the exhumation of Bernadette's body in St Joseph's Chapel on 22nd September 1909, which was thirty years after her death. This was an intrinsic part of the diocesan beatification process.

The wooden lid was unscrewed and the lead coffin was then cut open in the presence of a surgeon named Doctor Ch. David and a physician, Doctor A. Jourdan. Other people were also standing there to witness the exhumation, including Bishop Gauthey, several other religious people, the Mayor of Nevers and also the Deputy Mayor.

The first observation that the two doctors made was that there was absolutely no smell, which was highly unusual. They also observed that the habit that Bernadette was wearing was damp, the rosary that she was holding was rusty and the crucifix in her hands had turned green. This all indicated that there was a high degree of moisture in the environment of the vault of St Joseph's chapel.

Under normal circumstances, high moisture levels would have rapidly accelerated the decomposition of a corpse, but they were surprised to find that the body hadn't decayed at all.

Part of the doctor's statement, which was made under oath, was:

"The head was tilted to the left. The face was dull white. The skin clung to the muscles and the muscles adhered to the bones. The eye sockets were covered by the eyelids. The brows were flat on the skin and stuck to the arches above the eyes. The lashes of the right eyelid were stuck to the skin. The nose was dilated and shrunken. The mouth was open slightly and it could be seen that the teeth were still in place. The hands, which were crossed on her breast, were perfectly preserved, as were the nails. The hands still held a rusting rosary. The veins on the forearms stood out."

Bishop Gauthey said that the attitude of Bernadette in the coffin reminded him of the young Christian virgins that had been discovered in the Catacombs of Rome.

After the examination was completed, the nuns washed Bernadette's body and placed it in a new coffin which was lined with zinc and padded with white coloured silk.

So by 23rd October 1909, just 14 months after the first session was convened, the Sacred Congregation of Rites in Rome had received all the documentation from the Ecclesiastical Court in Nevers. This Congregation deals with the process of the canonisation of saints, as well as the supervision of the Liturgy and the Sacraments.

The Sacred Congregation of Rites then reviewed all the evidence into Bernadette's life to decide if there was a case for her to be declared 'Venerable.' This title can be given to people who have displayed heroic values in their lifetime. After the review, the Congregation then passed its recommendation through to the Pontiff for his approval.

So four years after the Ecclesiastical Court in Nevers had submitted all its evidence through to Rome, Pope Pius X finally signed the Decree for the Introduction of the Cause of Bernadette's beatification on 13th August 1913, giving Bernadette the title 'Venerable.'

The stage after being declared venerable is 'beatification' and this is a recognition by the Church of a person's entrance into Heaven and their capacity to intercede on behalf of individuals who pray in his or her name.

At that time, Cardinal Antonio Vico was the Prefect of the Sacred Congregation of Rites and so the next stage in the process of canonisation, known as the 'Apostolic Process,' fell under his authority.

Bishop Pierre Chatelus had been appointed Bishop of Nevers on 13th April 1910, after Bishop Gauthey had become Archbishop of Besancon, and so he would preside over the Apostolic Process concerning Bernadette at the diocesan level.

Unfortunately the outbreak of World War I delayed the start of this Commission by a few years, and the Apostolic Process only began on 17th September 1917. The Commission presided over by Bishop Chatelus would ultimately hold an astonishing 203 sessions in total.

Less than a month after the Apostolic Process began, on 13th October 1917 the incredible 'Miracle of the Sun' was witnessed by 70,000 people at Fatima in Portugal. Ten year old Lucia dos Santos and her young cousins Francisco and Jacinta Marto claimed to have witnessed six apparitions of the Virgin Mary between 13th May and 13th October of that year.

During the third apparition on 13th July, the children were given a terrifying vision of Hell, and they were warned that unless mankind ceased offending God through sin, then a war worse than World War I would break out during the pontificate of Pius XI.

They were told that the sign that the world was about to be chastised through war, famine, persecutions of the Church and the Holy Father would be a night illumined by an unknown light. The Virgin Mary said that to prevent this she would come to ask for the consecration of Russia to Her Immaculate Heart, as well as a new devotion - the Communion of Reparation on the First Five Saturdays.

She said that if her requests were met, then Russia would be converted, but if not, then Russia would spread her errors throughout the world, causing wars and persecutions of the Church. The good would be martyred, the Holy Father would have much to suffer, and various nations would be annihilated. However, she said that in the end, Her Immaculate Heart would triumph.

It was on 13th July 1917 that Mary gave another vision, which came to be known as the 'third secret' and she also told the children that she would give a sign in October of that year, so that all would believe. The Miracle of the Sun has never been satisfactorily explained by scientists to this day. The timing of the Virgin Mary's apparitions at Fatima, and her warning about Russia are quite remarkable, as she actually appeared during the Russian Revolution. White Russians would ultimately lose to the Bolshevics, who would then turn the nation into a communist state.

As part of its investigation, the Commission of Bishop Chatelus authorised a second exhumation of Bernadette's body, and this took place on 3rd April 1919, over nine years after the first exhumation.

Bishop Chatelus, the Commissioner of Police, members of the Church Tribunal, and representatives of the municipalities were all present as Doctors Comte and Talon inspected the body. As in the earlier exhumation, when the coffin was opened there was no odour and Bernadette's body was found to be absolutely intact.

This is part of Doctor Comte's report:

"At the request of the Bishop of Nevers I detached and removed the rear section of the fifth and sixth right ribs as relics; I noticed that there was a resistant, hard mass in the thorax, which was the liver covered by the diaphragm. I also took a piece of the diaphragm and the liver beneath it as relics, and can affirm that this organ was in a remarkable state of preservation. I also removed the two patella bones to which the skin clung and which were covered with more clinging calcium matter. Finally, I removed the muscle fragments right and left from the outsides of the thighs. These muscles were also in a very good state of preservation and did not seem to have putrefied at all."

"From this examination I conclude that the body of the Venerable Bernadette is intact, the skeleton is complete, the muscles have atrophied, but are well preserved; only the skin, which is shriveled, seems to have suffered from the effects of the damp in the coffin."

The Commission finally submitted all the documentation on Bernadette's case to the Congregation of Rites on 11th February 1920. But it took until 18th November 1923 for Pope Pius XI to publish the

'Decree on the heroic nature of the virtues of the Venerable Sister Marie-Bernard Soubirous.'

He announced this in the Sala Ducale (Ducal Hall) in the ancient Vatican Apostolic Palace, before speaking about Bernadette's sanctity. Part of his address was:

"There is no doubt that we are here in the presence of sanctity in the precise and exact meaning of the word.... In fact, when one considers Bernadette's life such as it appears at every stage of the Processes, which have been lengthy, careful, considered and strict, as they should always be, we are pleased to say, for the greater glory of God, this life can be summed up in three words: Bernadette was faithful to her mission, she was humble in glory, she was valiant under trial."

Now before beatification, the Pontiff needs to approve a miracle as evidence of the intercessory power of the venerable person. In Bernadette's case, ten claims of miraculous healings had been thoroughly investigated before being submitted to the Congregation of Rites, of which it selected two for consideration. Submissions by the doctors involved, as well as witness statements were examined over the course of three sittings of the Congregation of Rites.

One case involved Sister Marie-Melanie Meyer, of the Sisters of Providence of Ribeauville, who in 1910 was diagnosed with a gastric ulcer at the age of thirty. The ulcer caused her acute pain and she frequently vomited and was unable to eat.

Her condition deteriorated until she came close to death, at which point she decided to make a pilgrimage to Bernadette's tomb in the chapel at Nevers. She suffered terribly on the 59 kilometre journey from Moulins, but she made it to St Joseph's Chapel where she prayed at Bernadette's tomb for an hour.

Marie-Melanie's pain suddenly disappeared and she was then able to eat a meal without any difficulty at all, before returning to Moulins where the very next day she was able to return to her normal, pre-illness duties.

The other case was that of Henri Boisselet, who was struck down with tuberculous peritonitis in November 1913. This is a very serious condition that results from tuberculosis spreading to the peritoneum, which is a continuous membrane that lines the abdominal cavity and the abdominal organs.

He and other people began a novena to Bernadette, the ninth day of which was the 8th of December, and on that very day he was instantaneously and permanently cured.

The next year he even went to the Western Front with the French Army, where he was captured and then marched back to Germany as a prisoner of war. Despite living in poor conditions in captivity for two years and eight months, he returned home to France in good health.

The third and final exhumation of Bernadette's remains took place on 18th April 1925, when Doctor Comte was asked to take more relics from her body. This is part of his report:

"What struck me during this examination, of course, was the state of perfect preservation of the skeleton, the fibrous tissues of the muscles (still supple and firm), of the ligaments, and of the skin, and above all the totally unexpected state of the liver after 46 years.

"One would have thought that this organ, which is basically soft and inclined to crumble, would have decomposed very rapidly or would have hardened to a chalky consistency. Yet, when it was cut it was soft and almost normal in consistency. I pointed this out to those present, remarking that this did not seem to be a natural phenomenon."

After Doctor Comte had completed his examination and the removal of parts of Bernadette's body, he had her body swathed in bandages, but he left her face and hands free.

By then it had been decided that Bernadette's body would be put on display and so Pierre Imans of Paris, who made wax mannequins for department stores, made a light wax mask from an imprint of Bernadette's face and hands. This was because although there'd been no decomposition of her face or body, there was a blackish discolouration of the skin of her face and her eyes were sunken.

On 1st May 1925, the Decree of Miracle was read out by Pope Pius XI which acknowledged that these two miracles were genuine and valid for the Cause of Bernadette.

Then on 2nd June, Pius XI declared by Apostolic Decree in the Consistorial Hall, that Bernadette could in all security be proclaimed 'Blessed.'

There was a huge gathering in St Peter's Basilica in Rome on the morning of Sunday 14th June to hear Cardinal Rafael Merry del Val have the Brief of Beatification read out.

Reverend Mother Bordenave of St Gildard's Convent in Nevers was there with a large contingent of her nuns. The announcement was greeted with tremendous applause that at last, Bernadette had officially and publically been declared 'Blessed.'

After Beatification, the Church requires another miracle for the scientific and the theological commissions of the Congregation for the Causes of the Saints to consider. The two commissions didn't have to wait long for their miracle, and it couldn't have occurred at a more appropriate time either!

Bernadette's body was placed in a crystal coffin, which went on display on 3rd August 1925 in St Joseph's Chapel in the grounds of the Convent in Nevers.

Now, Bishop Lemaitre of Carthage was one of the people due to attend the ceremony of the translation (moving) of Bernadette's reliquary that day. He'd been suffering for over ten years from a debilitating amoebic infection that he'd contracted while working in various tropical countries, and all attempts at treatment had failed, so that his doctors had now said that there was no hope of a cure.

Even during his journey from Paris to Nevers that day, he had another serious attack, but was still able to make the ceremony of translation, but during that ceremony he was instantaneously healed. He was even able to resume his ministry in Carthage and live a normal, healthy life.

The second miraculous cure referred to the Congregation for the Causes of the Saints involved Sister Marie de Saint-Fidele of Lourdes, who'd suffered with dorso-lumbar Potts' Disease and a tumour on her knee. The disease progressed to the point where she became an invalid and her doctors declared that a cure was impossible.

A Novena of prayers was made to Bernadette, and on the fifth day, 6th February 1928 at 6pm, Sister Marie felt in herself that she'd been cured. The next morning she was even able to get out of bed after having been bedridden for such a long time. Medical specialists conducted thorough examinations of Sister Marie but found absolutely no trace of the disease anywhere in her body.

The Congregation carefully examined the two reported miracles and then submitted their recommendations through to the Pontiff. On Wednesday 31st May 1933, the Decree of Approbation of the Miracles was read in the Vatican Palace before Pope Pius XI.

Then on Sunday 2nd July, which is the Feast of the Virgin Mary's visitation, the Decree de Tuto was finally published. The long and arduous road to Bernadette's canonisation had taken just short of 25 years from the day that Bishop Gauthey had first constituted the Ecclesiastical Court in Nevers!

On Friday 8th December 1933, appropriately being the Feast of the Immaculate Conception, Pope Pius XI declared Blessed Marie-Bernard Soubirous a saint in St Peter's Basilica. He also announced that the 16th of April, the date on which she had died, would be her Feast day in the Church calendar.

The surviving members of the Soubirous family were there, as was the Very Reverend Mother Crapard, the Superior General of the Sisters of Charity of Nevers, along with 160 of her nuns.

About ten thousand people had made the journey from France to be at the mass that day, and there were about forty thousand people in the naves of the Basilica. Eighteen Cardinals and eighty-five Bishops, Archbishops and Patriarchs were also in attendance.

In his homily, the pope emphasised the humility of Bernadette, saying that she was a simple miller's daughter who possessed no other wealth other than the candour of her exquisite soul.

Sadly Archbishop Gauthey had passed away on 25th July 1918 during World War I and wasn't there to see Bernadette's canonisation being announced by the Pope.

But two people were standing there that day who'd been pieces in the amazing jigsaw puzzle of the road to her becoming a saint. One of them was Bishop Lemaitre, the man who'd been healed at St Joseph's Chapel in Nevers on 3rd August 1925.

The other is utterly remarkable. It was 77 year old Justin Bouhort, who as a dying infant had been held under the water at Massabielle for fifteen minutes by his mother, before being miraculously healed of his tuberculosis 75 years earlier, in July 1858.

The huge crowds visiting Lourdes ultimately prompted the construction of the Basilica of St Pius X, known as the Underground Basilica, which was completed in 1958 (the 100th anniversary) and which has a capacity of 25,000.

Another place of worship, the Church of St Bernadette, was built on the other side of the river to the grotto in 1988, on the very spot where Bernadette stood during the 18th and final Apparition.

Later, in 1996, the six storey Accueil Notre Dame was built, which provides accommodation for the sick pilgrims who are visiting Lourdes.

Since 1858 there have been around 7,000 miraculous healings reported, and the Church has verified 70 of them after rigorous examination of the evidence by the Medical Bureau of the Sanctuary of Lourdes. They include cases of people being cured of cancer, multiple sclerosis, paralysis, and blindness.

An example is that of Vittorio Micheli, who was diagnosed with a malignant tumour of his left hip, at a hospital in Verona on 4th June 1962. His condition deteriorated severely over the next year, resulting in the complete destruction of his hip joint. Vittorio made a pilgrimage to Lourdes in June 1963, and he bathed in the water with a plaster cast on, that extended from his pelvis down to his foot. Soon after his return home, Vittorio's condition improved, the pain subsided, and he was later able to walk again. Further x-rays were taken which revealed "the remarkable reconstruction of his hip" without Vittorio having had any medical intervention. On 26th May 1976, 13 years after the cure, Monsignor Alessandro Gottardi declared that the healing contained "sufficient evidence for the recognition of a special intervention by the Power of God, Father and Creator."

It's clear that given the extreme caution taken by the Lourdes Medical Bureau and the Church, it's likely that there have been far more miracles than the 70 officially recognised ones. It's estimated that since the Apparitions of 1858, about 200 million people have visited Lourdes.

When studying the events at Lourdes and the life of Bernadette, one of the striking things is that the Virgin Mary chose to appear to such an innocent and simple girl.

In our society, we tend to rate a person by their looks, their status, intelligence and material wealth, unlike God who looks to the heart, and an example of this was God choosing David, a young and unassuming young man, to become the King of Israel.

1 Samuel 16:7: But the Lord said to Samuel, "Do not consider his appearance or his height, for I have rejected him. The Lord does not look at the things man looks at. Man looks at the outward appearance, but the Lord looks at the heart."

There are strong parallels here with God Himself choosing the Virgin Mary for a unique role in developing his relationship with Mankind, and Bernadette herself recognised this.

On 4th July 1866, the day she said farewell to her family and left for Nevers, Bernadette said, "Yes, dear Mother, you have come down to the earth to appear to a weak child. You, Queen of heaven and earth, have chosen what was the most humble according to the world."

On another occasion she said, "I was nothing, and of this nothing God made something great."

When the Virgin Mary, who was pregnant with Jesus at the time, visited her relative Elizabeth in Judea, she praised God in a prayer we call the Magnificat. It starts: **"My soul glorifies the Lord and my spirit rejoices in God my Saviour, for he has been mindful of the humble state of his servant."**

At Lourdes, Mary brought hope to a people suffering through poverty and disease, uplifting them spiritually and rekindling their faith.

But there are two timeless messages for mankind in the story of Lourdes. The first is that Mary is the Immaculate Conception, and the second is her call to repentance. If we trust Mary as our most powerful intercessor to Jesus, she will be able to help us along the path to his love, and to eternal life.

Chapter 5

God's plan for Mankind

To appreciate the significance of Mary appearing to Bernadette at Lourdes, we first need to understand God's plan for mankind and then look at Mary's role within that plan.

Created in God's image

It's clear from Genesis that man was created in a unique way, in that he actually shares some elements of the essence of God, most notably that we have an immortal soul and a spiritual nature.

Genesis 1:26: Then God said, "Let us make man in our image, in our likeness …."

So as human beings, we're different to all other forms of life on earth as we have the unique capacity to form a relationship with our Creator. As our souls live on after physical death, God's plan is for each of us to spend eternity as transformed, resurrected beings living in His presence and immersed in His love, and this is known as the beatific vision.

Now although our intelligence is clearly far greater than any other species, the human mind has a distinct weakness, and that's a difficulty in comprehending very large or very small values, including the concept of eternity.

Take for example the sheer scale of our universe. Just our galaxy, the Milky Way, is thought to contain at least 100 billion stars, with the closest one being Proxima Centauri, which is 4.2 light years away.

Light travels at 300,000 kilometres per second, and yet it still takes 4.2 years for light from our closest star (apart from the sun) to reach us. So this means that the closest star to earth is 40 trillion kilometres away!

Research from NASA's Hubble telescope and other observatories around the earth indicates that there are at least 100 billion galaxies (not stars) just in the observable part of the cosmos!

So, as human beings, we find it immensely difficult to comprehend orders of magnitude like this, as well as any notion of what it's like to live for eternity.

Jesus had often spoken to his apostles about the incredible joy that resurrected souls would experience in heaven, but he knew that they were struggling to visualise it. And it was perhaps for this reason that he took his most trusted companions, Peter, James and John, up a high mountain to show them the magnificence of a resurrected body at the transfiguration.

Jesus was possibly alluding to the transfiguration in something he said to his apostles eight days before this startling event, because he said that some of them would see the kingdom of God while they were still alive.

Luke 9:27: "I tell you the truth, some who are standing here will not taste death before they see the kingdom of God."

About eight days after Jesus said this, he took Peter, John and James with him and went up onto a mountain to pray. As he was praying, the appearance of his face changed, and his clothes became as bright as a flash of lightning.

Two men, Moses and Elijah appeared in glorious splendour, talking with Jesus. They spoke about his departure, which he was about to bring to fulfillment at Jerusalem. Peter and his companions were very sleepy, but when they became fully awake, they saw his glory and the two men standing with him.

As the men were leaving Jesus, Peter said to him, "Master, it is good for us to be here. Let us put up three shelters – one for you, one for Moses and one for Elijah." (He did not know what he was saying.)

While he was speaking, a cloud appeared and enveloped them, and they were afraid as they entered the cloud. A voice came from the cloud, saying, "This is my Son, whom I have chosen; listen to him." When the voice had spoken, they found that Jesus was alone.

In Matthew's account of the transfiguration, he wrote: 'His face shone like the sun, and his clothes became as white as the light.'

At the transfiguration, Jesus wanted his apostles to see the sheer glory of the risen body as it would help them to understand the nature of life after death. This would focus their minds and help them to endure the trials that they would all endure as evangelists after his death.

On this mountain, the three apostles witnessed two characters from history who'd been dead for many hundreds of years, vibrantly alive and talking with Jesus and this must have been shattering and utterly life-changing for them!

Had the transfiguration of Jesus not happened, they wouldn't have been able to comprehend the nature of a risen body, and this wonderful event also shows us the glory that awaits all those who die in God's love, who will inherit eternal life as a reward.

When Jesus explained the Parable of the Weeds to his disciples he ended by saying that 'the righteous will shine like the sun' and so this comment also indicates the brilliance of the resurrected body.

Matthew 13:41: "The Son of Man will send out his angels, and they will weed out of his kingdom everything that causes sin and all who do evil. They will throw them into the fiery furnace, where there will be weeping and gnashing of teeth. Then the righteous will shine like the sun in the kingdom of their father."

A little further on in his gospel, Matthew quotes what Jesus said about people being rewarded for showing love to those who are in need, and again he refers to the afterlife.

This reading also shows that it was God's plan from the very beginning for us not just to have a physical existence which ends at death, but an eternal, glorious life in heaven as well.

Matthew 25:31: "When the Son of Man comes in his glory, and all the angels with him, he will sit on his throne in heavenly glory. All the nations will be gathered before him, and he will separate the people one from another as a shepherd separates the sheep from the goats. He will put the sheep on his right and the goats on his left.

"Then the King will say to those on his right, 'Come, you who are blessed my Father; take your inheritance, the kingdom prepared for you since the creation of the world. For I was hungry and you gave me something to eat, I was thirsty and you gave me

something to drink, I was a stranger and you invited me in, I needed clothes and you clothed me, I was sick and you looked after me, I was in prison and you came to visit me.'"

And we get another glimpse of the nature of the afterlife from an interaction between the Sadducees and Jesus, when they tried to trap him on the issue of whether there was indeed a life after death.

Luke 20:27: Some of the Sadducees, who say there is no resurrection, came to Jesus with a question.

"Teacher," they said, "Moses wrote for us that if a man's brother dies and leaves a wife but no children, the man must marry the widow and have children for his brother. Now there were seven brothers. The first one married a woman and died childless. The second and then the third married her, and in the same way the seven died, leaving no children. Finally, the woman died too. Now then, at the resurrection whose wife will she be, since the seven were married to her?"

Jesus replied, "The people of this age marry and are given in marriage. But those who are considered worthy of taking part in that age and in the resurrection from the dead will neither marry nor be given in marriage, and they can no longer die; for they are like the angels. They are God's children, since they are children of the resurrection.

"But in the account of the burning bush, even Moses showed that the dead rise, for he calls the Lord 'the God of Abraham, and the God of Isaac, and the God of Jacob.' He is not the God of the dead, but of the living, for to him all are alive."

Of the three groups of Jews, the Sadducees, the Pharisees and the Essenes, it was the Sadducees who didn't believe in a life after death at all, and so here Jesus corrects them on their false teaching.

Resurrected beings will clearly have no desire for sex, nor any need for procreation or marriage, and will be like the angels in this regard. Disease, accidents, ageing and death will not exist in the kingdom that God has prepared for those who are worthy of eternal life.

So the life that God originally intended for man, which was withdrawn from him due to the disobedience of sin, will be fully restored in heaven. The all consuming love that we will feel from being in such close proximity to God will mean that any desire for other resurrected souls will be quite impossible. There will be a quantum leap in knowledge and power which will be transformational and which will raise us to the level of angelic beings.

Saint Paul also described the glory that awaits those who die in God's love in his first letter to the Christian community of Corinth in Greece.

1 Corinthians 2:9: "No eye has seen, no ear has heard, no mind has conceived what God has prepared for those who love him."

1 Corinthians 15:42: "So will it be with the resurrection of the dead. The body that is sown is perishable, it is raised imperishable; it is sown in dishonour, it is raised in glory; it is sown in weakness, it is raised in power; it is sown a natural body, it is raised a spiritual body."

1 Corinthians 15:51: "Listen, I tell you a mystery: We will not all sleep, but we will all be changed – in a flash, in the twinkling of an eye, at the last trumpet. For the trumpet will sound, the dead will be raised imperishable, and we will be changed. For the perishable must clothe itself with the imperishable, and the mortal with immortality."

The rift caused by sin

So the above readings show us the unimaginable joy that souls will experience in heaven, but unfortunately it's also clear from Scripture that not everyone will inherit eternal life.

An example of this is found in **Matthew 7:13**, where Jesus said: **"Enter through the narrow gate. For wide is the gate and broad is the road that leads to destruction, and many enter through it. But small is the gate and narrow the road that leads to life, and only a few find it."**

A little further on, in **Matthew 7:21** Jesus is quoted as saying, **"Not everyone who says to me, 'Lord, Lord,' will enter the kingdom of heaven, but only he who does the will of my Father who is in heaven."**

Now Paul described how sin is an innate part of the human condition in Romans 3:23 when he wrote, **"for all have sinned and fall short of the glory of God."**

So it's clear that **obedience** to His will is key critical if we are to live out our lives in a way that's pleasing to God and so inherit the unimaginable joys of heaven.

The stigmatist priest Padre Pio summed it up nicely when he wrote:

'Where there is no obedience, there is no virtue; where there is no virtue there is no good; where there is no good, there is no love; where there is no love, there is no God; and where there is no God, there is no Paradise.'

God gave every human being the gift of 'free will' and so He doesn't force us to believe in Him, nor dictate how we live and act, but rather He allows us the complete freedom to make all these choices for ourselves.

When we look at the story of the Fall of Man in Genesis, we can see that God had provided every possible thing necessary for the sustenance and happiness of man. But despite this, man was disobedient to the will of God and he put aside his love for his Creator and yielded to temptation.

Genesis 2:15: And the Lord God commanded the man, "You are free to eat from any tree in the garden; but you must not eat from the tree of the knowledge of good and evil, for when you eat of it you will surely die."

Genesis 3:1: Now the serpent was more crafty than any of the wild animals the Lord God had made. He said to the woman, "Did God really say, 'You must not eat from any tree in the garden?'"

The woman said to the serpent, "We may eat fruit from the trees in the garden, but God did say, 'You must not eat fruit from the tree that is in the middle of the garden, and you must not touch it, or you will die.'"

"You will not surely die," the serpent said to the woman. "For God knows that when you eat of it your eyes will be opened, and you will be like God, knowing good and evil."

When the woman saw that the fruit of the tree was good for food and pleasing to the eye, and also desirable for gaining wisdom, she took some and ate it. She also gave some to her husband, who was with her, and he ate it. Then the eyes of both of them were opened, and they realised they were naked; so they sewed fig leaves together and made coverings for themselves.

Then the man and his wife heard the sound of the Lord God as he was walking in the garden in the cool of the day, and they hid from the Lord God among the trees of the garden.

But the Lord God called to the man, "Where are you?"

He answered, "I heard you in the garden, and I was afraid because I was naked; so I hid."

And he said, "Who told you that you were naked? Have you eaten from the tree from which I commanded you not to eat?"

The man said, "The woman you put here with me – she gave me some fruit from the tree, and I ate it."

Then the Lord God said to the woman, "What is this you have done?"

The woman said, "The serpent deceived me, and I ate."

So the Lord God said to the serpent, "Because you have done this, 'cursed are you above all the livestock and all the wild animals! You will crawl on your belly and you will eat dust all the days of your life. And I will put enmity between you and the woman, and between your offspring and hers; he will crush your head, and you will strike his heel."

To the woman he said, "I will greatly increase your pains in childbearing; with pain you will give birth to children. Your desire will be for your husband, and he will rule over you."

To Adam he said, "Because you listened to your wife and ate from the tree about which I commanded you, 'You must not eat of it,' cursed is the ground because of you; through painful toil you will eat of it all the days of your life.

"It will produce thorns and thistles for you, and you will eat the plants of the field. By the sweat of your brow you will eat your food until you return to the ground, since from it you were taken; for dust you are and to dust you will return."

Adam named his wife Eve, because she would become the mother of all the living.

The Lord God made garments of skin for Adam and his wife and clothed them. And the Lord God said, "The man has now become like one of us, knowing good and evil. He must not be allowed to reach out his hand and take also from the tree of life and eat, and live for ever." So the Lord God banished him from the Garden of Eden to work the ground from which he had been taken.

Now this story beautifully illustrates a few points. Firstly, as human beings we have a highly inquisitive nature which tests the boundaries of the environment and the situations that we find ourselves in.

Secondly, we're inclined to want far more in life than what we actually need, and are easily tempted by the allure of various things such as wealth, power and sex. In the Genesis account, Adam and Eve clearly didn't need the fruit from that tree at all, but they still took it anyway!

Another point that emerges is that we all have a conscience which allows us to instinctively know when we're about to do something wrong. In the Genesis story, we can see the woman's conscience at play as she debates with the serpent whether or not it would actually be wrong for her to eat the fruit.

This story also shows that our earthly life is a test of our love for God, because if we genuinely love Him then we'll be obedient to His will, and this is clear from what Jesus himself said on the subject.

John 14:23: Jesus replied, "If anyone loves me, he will obey my teaching. My Father will love him, and we will come to him and make our home with him. He who does not love me will not obey my teaching. These words you hear are not my own; they belong to the Father who sent me."

A further point is that we all have the capacity to resist temptation, but we're also able to rationalise committing a sin in our minds before yielding to it. We put aside the moral argument against doing something we know is instinctively wrong, in favour of getting the benefit derived from a given action.

Another lesson from the story is that there are three, not two parties at play which influence our decision to sin or not to sin. God's commands are clear, and we intuitively know by our conscience if something we are about to do is inherently wrong or not.

The third party in this is the Devil or Satan, whose objectives are diametrically opposed to those of a loving God, and whose sole motivation is to draw us away from His love, thereby denying us the glory of eternal life in heaven.

Matthew and Luke's gospels show us that even Jesus was sorely tempted in the wilderness when he was at his weakest, after having fasted for 40 days. Satan tempted Jesus with a physical craving (tell these stones to become bread), by inciting Jesus to put God to the test (throw yourself down from the highest point of the temple), and with the lure of wealth and power (I will give you all the kingdoms of the world).

But we can take comfort from the fact that, just as Jesus was able to resist all three of these temptations, we also have the ability to do so. Jesus succeeded in doing this by using counter arguments to each of the temptations, and crucially, by bringing God into the equation each time.

He fought the temptation to turn stones into bread by saying, "Man does not live on bread alone, but on every word that comes from the mouth of God." He countered the desire to test God by saying, "Do not put the Lord your God to the test." And he negated the lust for power, which is essentially making 'gods' of material things, by replying, "Worship the Lord your God, and serve him only."

In our modern world, which has made huge scientific advances that allow for most things to be analysed and quantified, it's all too easy to forget the existence of true evil, and the manifestation of this in Satan and the fallen angels which exist all around us.

The Genesis story also shows us that there are consequences to sin, and that while we avoid sin and live in a state of grace, we remain in communion and harmony with our God. However, when we disobey his commands, we inevitably pull ourselves away from that communion with Him, and we then live a compromised spiritual existence on earth, and risk losing our eternal life in heaven. It also shows that the long term spiritual damage done far outweighs the short term physical benefit derived from giving into any sin.

However, what's important to remember is that despite man having sinned, the love that God had for his creation remained unchanged, hence He still made clothes for them after the fall. So we should never forget that our Creator is a God of love, compassion and forgiveness above all else. In the story we can see that the disobedience of man to the will of God created a fracture in our relationship with Him, and so man was banned from the Garden of Eden, where he'd previously lived in close proximity to God. Man became mortal as a result of this, and the thorns and thistles in the Genesis story represent the diseases and the pests that afflict our bodies and our crops.

The importance of covenant

Nothing is more essential to our relationship with God than covenant, and the most important of these is the covenant instituted by Jesus at the Last Supper.

When we look at the structure of anything that God has created, from atoms to galaxies, or even at a tiny molecule of DNA, it's evident that there's order and stability throughout His creation. The importance of order is also evident in the covenants that God has made with Man, such as the Decalogue, or Ten Commandments. These are a recipe for stability in our relationship with God, with our spouse, with our neighbour, in the judiciary, and in society in general.

By keeping God's covenant, we honour Him and remain in His love, but by breaking that covenant, we offend Him and create discord. An example of the rewards which come from obeying the will of God can be found in the account of God asking Abraham to sacrifice his son Isaac.

Now since the time of the Patriarchs it had been a custom to offer a young male animal as a sin offering to God, as by giving up something of value it showed that a person had repented of their sins. Abraham had been asked by God to sacrifice his son Isaac as a test of his faith and obedience, and although it made absolutely no sense to Abraham, he was still prepared to carry out God's will.

Genesis 22:1: Some time later God tested Abraham. He said to him, "Abraham!"

"Here I am," he replied.

"Take your son, your only son, Isaac, whom you love, and go to the region of Moriah. Sacrifice him there as a burnt offering on one of the mountains I will tell you about."

Early the next morning Abraham got up and saddled his donkey. He took with him two of his servants and his son Isaac. When he had cut enough wood for the burnt offering, he set out for the place God had told him about. On the third day Abraham looked up and saw the place in the distance.

He said to his servants, "Stay here with the donkey while I and the boy go over there. We will worship and then we will come back to you." Abraham took the wood for the burnt offering and placed it on his son Isaac, and he himself carried the fire and the knife. As the two of them went on together, Isaac spoke up and said to his father Abraham, "Father?"

"Yes, my son?" Abraham replied.

"The fire and wood are here," Isaac said, "but where is the lamb for the burnt offering?"

Abraham answered, "God himself will provide the lamb for the burnt offering my son." And the two of them went on together. When they reached the place God had told him about, Abraham built an altar there and arranged the wood on it.

He bound his son Isaac and laid him on the altar, on top of the wood. Then he reached out his hand and took the knife to slay his son. But the angel of the Lord called out to him from heaven, "Abraham! Abraham!"

"Here I am," he replied.

"Do not lay a hand on the boy," he said. "Do not do anything to him. Now I know that you fear God, because you have not withheld from me your son, your only son."

Abraham looked up and there in a thicket he saw a ram caught by its horns. He went over and took the ram and sacrificed it as a

burnt offering instead of his son. So Abraham called that place The Lord Will Provide. And to this day it is said, "On the mountain of the Lord it will be provided."

The angel of the Lord called to Abraham from heaven a second time and said, "I swear by myself, declares the Lord, that because you have done this and have not withheld your son, your only son, I will surely bless you and make your descendants as numerous as the stars in the sky and as the sand on the seashore. Your descendants will take possession of the cities of their enemies, and through your offspring all nations on earth will be blessed, because you have obeyed me."

Now there are strong parallels between this account of Abraham and Isaac, and with the sacrifice of Jesus, God's only son, where Jesus also carried the wood for the sacrifice on his back to Calvary. However, unlike in the case of Isaac, God did allow his son to be sacrificed as a sin offering, to redeem the sins of many.

God entered into various covenants with the Israelites, but again and again these were broken, with disastrous consequences. An example was when Moses was given the two stone tablets inscribed with the Ten Commandments on Mount Sinai, and these Commandments formed the covenant between God and the Israelites.

The commandments were a simple and effective way of giving laws to everyone regardless of their level of education, and they ensured that society remained in an orderly state.

The second census of the Israelites wandering in the desert gave a population of 601,730 men over the age of twenty and in addition to this there were 23,000 male Levites aged one month and older. If we were to include women and those under the age of twenty, then we would surely have a figure of a few million Israelites!

To control this population that lacked the infrastructure and administration of a large city and that was often on the move, meant that a strict code of rules and observances had to be devised. So the Ten Commandments were an ideal core of rules to ensure stability and cohesion in this nomadic society.

But it didn't take long before the Israelites rebelled against God by melting down the gold they'd taken out of Egypt to form an idol of a calf, which they then worshipped. Of course by doing this they'd broken the commandment, 'You shall have no other Gods before me.'"

However, the tribe of Levi refused to worship this idol and so God blessed the Levites for staying true to His covenant.

Exodus 32:29: Then Moses said, "You have been set apart to the Lord today, for you were against your own sons and brothers, and he has blessed you this day."

As punishment for breaking the covenant by worshipping the idol, about three thousand Israelites were killed that day, and so here we see a recurring theme, where God punishes those who break His covenant and where He rewards those who hold true to it.

Now God sent many prophets from the time of Moses through to the latter day prophets such as Zechariah, in an attempt to draw man away from sin and to His love and to true spirituality. But unfortunately the response to the message of these prophets was short lived and the vast majority of them were martyred.

Over time, the interpretation of the Commandments gradually developed into a staggering code of 613 Mitzvot (observances), of which 365 were negative and 248 were positive instructions. The Jews now thought that they were worshipping God by rigorously following these hundreds of man-made rules, but the core values of God, which are compassion, love and mercy, had somehow been lost from the code as it had evolved.

The covenant of Jesus

Without God's intervention, mankind seemed destined to stray ever further from His love and to the hope of securing eternal life. Sending yet more prophets wouldn't present an ongoing solution, and so God found it necessary to intervene directly by sending His son Jesus into the world two thousand years ago.

Now it's important for us to remember that Jesus and the Holy Spirit existed with God the Father at the beginning of time, and that they were intrinsically involved in the creation of the universe. This is clear from the beginning of John's gospel where Jesus is called 'The Word' and also in Genesis where the plural 'we' and 'us' are used and where the 'Spirit of God' is mentioned.

Genesis 1:1: In the beginning God created the heavens and the earth. Now the earth was formless and empty, darkness was over the surface of the deep, and the Spirit of God was hovering over the waters.

Genesis 1:26: Then God said, "Let us make man in our image, in our likeness …."

John 1:1: In the beginning was the Word, and the Word was with God, and the Word was God. He was with God in the beginning. Through him all things were made; without him nothing was made that has been made.

In fact, Jesus himself stated that he was with God before creation, as is clear from **John 17:4: "And now, Father, glorify me in your presence with the glory I had with you before the world began."**

The timing of this intervention, i.e. Jesus becoming incarnate on earth, was critically important, because had this been done too early in man's history then the message might not have spread worldwide, as the world would have been too sparsely populated.

Had the intervention been made too late, then many more souls would not have inherited eternal life. So it made sense for Jesus to become incarnate at the time he did, because by then there were established languages, towns and international trade routes, but the world population was still low.

A new, permanent covenant was also required, and so God allowed His only son to be offered up as a sacrifice on the cross at the end of his three year ministry. This incomprehensible outpouring of love would redeem the sins of those who accept him as the Christ, and so restore their fractured relationship with God.

However, the establishment of this new covenant doesn't mean that the Ten Commandments have become redundant, and Jesus was at pains to point this out.

Matthew 5:17: Do not think that I have come to abolish the Law or the Prophets; I have not come to abolish them but to fulfill them. I tell you the truth, until heaven and earth disappear, not

the smallest letter, not the least stroke of a pen, will by any means disappear from the Law until everything is accomplished.

Jesus waited until the night before his crucifixion to announce this new and everlasting covenant at the Last Supper in Jerusalem.

Matthew 26:26: While they were eating, Jesus took bread, gave thanks and broke it, and gave it to his disciples, saying, "Take and eat; this is my body."

Then he took the cup, gave thanks and offered it to them, saying, "Drink from it, all of you. This is my blood of the covenant, which is poured out for many for the forgiveness of sins. I tell you, I will not drink of this fruit of the vine from now on until that day when I drink it anew with you in my Father's kingdom."

Now covenants involve two parties, and both sides must comply with their obligations in order for the covenant to remain valid, such as in the covenant of marriage where there's an ongoing requirement for fidelity by both partners.

Our part of the covenant is to be baptised and to believe that Jesus is indeed the Son of God. By having this faith, we become a party to the new covenant in his death and resurrection, and so receive the reward of that covenant, which is eternal life.

So, in summary we can see that God created us to be unique of all life forms on earth, as we are spiritual beings made in His image and having the capacity to relate with Him. God's plan has always been for us to live a time-limited physical existence on earth, but later to be raised from death and transformed, so that we can then live for all eternity in His presence.

But mankind has a propensity to disobey God's will through sin, which under normal circumstances would have rendered all of us incapable of ever going to heaven. However, the new covenant that God established through His son has redeemed the sins of all those who accept Jesus as the Christ and made their salvation possible.

The Virgin Mary was an intrinsic and essential part of God's plan to establish this covenant, as it was only through the unique qualities of Mary that Jesus could have become incarnate in our world in the first place.

- Chapter 6 -

Mary, The Immaculate Conception

In this chapter we'll look at the qualities of Mary that made it possible for her to carry Jesus in her womb, and at her ongoing role in drawing us to the love of God.

It's surely no coincidence that Mary chose to appear at Lourdes so soon after the doctrine of the Immaculate Conception had been declared an infallible teaching of the Church by Pope Pius IX in 1854. It's also remarkable that Mary revealed to Bernadette that she was the Immaculate Conception on 25th March 1858, which of all days in the Church calendar is the Feast Day of The Annunciation! This was when the Angel Gabriel announced to Mary that she would conceive through the power of the Holy Spirit and carry the Son of God in her womb.

So this declaration by Our Lady at Lourdes can logically be seen as her endorsement of this teaching of the Church. Appreciating the significance of the Immaculate Conception is critical to us understanding the unique position that Mary holds of all human beings, and how she's an intrinsic part of God's plan to draw us all to His love.

Pope Pius IX defined this teaching in 1854 when he wrote:

"We declare, pronounce and define that the doctrine which holds that the Blessed Virgin Mary, at the first instant of her conception, by a singular privilege and grace of the Omnipotent God, in virtue of the merits of Jesus Christ, the Saviour of mankind, was preserved immaculate from all stain of original sin, has been revealed by God, and therefore should firmly and constantly be believed by all the faithful."

According to both Christian and Islamic tradition, the mother of the Virgin Mary was Anne, and she's mentioned in the apocryphal Gospel of James which was written in Greek around 150 AD, and the text also mentions Anne's husband, Joachim of Nazareth.

Another teaching of the Church is the **Perpetual Virginity of Mary** and here there's been some contention about the mention in the Gospels of Jesus having had brothers, but this is simply down to etymology. The Old Testament was written in Hebrew and in this language there's no word equivalent to the English words for cousin or nephew and so they're all described as being brothers.

Now the Greek word for brother is 'adelphos,' which is a union of 'a' for same and 'delph' for womb. So when the Old Testament writings were translated into Greek, the translators used the word 'adelphos' to describe brother, but this word was also used to describe a cousin or a nephew. Later, the authors of the New Testament, who wrote mainly in Greek from outset, continued to use the word adelphos in this way. And so the brothers mentioned were not sons of Mary, but rather other relatives of Jesus, and as Saint Jerome taught in the 5th century, they were most probably his cousins.

A small part of the New Testament was originally written in Aramaic and here again we have the same problem, as the Aramaic word for brother is 'aha' but this word is also used to describe other relatives such as cousins.

The translation of the first five books of the Old Testament (Torah) from Hebrew into Koine Greek is thought to have been completed during the 3rd century BC in Alexandria. The Greek translation of these Hebrew Scriptures is known as the Septuagint, or 'translation of the seventy' because 70 (or possibly 72) Jewish scribes were assembled for the task. Each scribe had to work independently of the others, and the texts had to be letter perfect or else they were discarded.

The question could be asked why it was necessary for the mother of the Christ to be completely devoid of sin. To answer that question, we only need to look at the history of the Israelites wandering in the desert, as this shows us that nothing imperfect can exist with God. We know this because when God was present on Mount Sinai, He warned Moses not to allow anyone to come near His presence.

Exodus 19:12: Put limits for the people around the mountain and tell them, 'Be careful that you do not go up the mountain or touch the foot of it. Whoever touches the mountain shall surely be put to death.'

Exodus 33:19: "I will have mercy on whom I will have mercy, and I will have compassion on whom I will have compassion." "But,"

he said, "You cannot see my face, for no one may see me and live."

Another way of viewing this is to say that it's physically impossible for God to be in the presence of anything which is imperfect. An analogy might be when you take two very powerful magnets and try to push the ends of the magnets with the same polarity together. It just cannot happen, as the magnets simply repel each other.

Yet despite God being perfect and man being inherently sinful, He still wanted to unite Himself with His creation in the most intimate and loving way possible, which was by allowing His divine Son Jesus to become man. This shows the depth of love that God has for us in that He was prepared to allow Jesus to assume the lowly condition of a human being, with all its inherent vulnerability. Jesus would therefore experience the full range of emotions, dangers and temptations that we all do in our day to day lives.

However, although Jesus became man, he would still always retain his divinity, and appreciating this is critical to understanding why Mary had to be immaculate. Mary being devoid of sin was the only environment in which the mutually exclusive entities of a perfect God, and man, could co-exist. Quite simply the conception of Jesus would have been impossible if it were not for this unique quality of Mary!

Matthew's gospel mentions an angel appearing to Joseph in a dream after he'd discovered that Mary was pregnant, and the angel explained to him that what had been conceived in Mary's womb was through divine intervention.

Matthew 1:20: But after he had considered this, an angel of the Lord appeared to him in a dream and said, "Joseph, son of David, do not be afraid to take Mary home as your wife, because what is conceived in her is from the Holy Spirit. She will give birth to a son, and you are to give him the name Jesus, because he will save his people from their sins."

Now in Luke's gospel we read of the appearance of the Angel Gabriel to Mary in Nazareth and of the conversation that they had.

Luke 1:26: In the sixth month, God sent the angel Gabriel to Nazareth, a town in Galilee, to a virgin pledged to be married to a man named Joseph, a descendent of David. The virgin's name

was Mary. The angel went to her and said, "Greetings, you who are highly favoured! The Lord is with you."

Mary was greatly troubled at his words and wondered what kind of greeting this might be. But the angel said to her, "Do not be afraid, Mary, you have found favour with God. You will be with child and give birth to a son, and you are to give him the name Jesus. He will be great and will be called the Son of the Most High. The Lord God will give him the throne of his father David, and he will reign over the house of Jacob for ever; his kingdom will never end."

"How will this be," Mary asked the angel, "since I am a virgin?"

The angel answered, "The Holy Spirit will come upon you and the power of the Most High will over-shadow you. So the holy one to be born will be called the Son of God. Even Elizabeth your relative is going to have a child in her old age, and she who was said to be barren is in her sixth month. For nothing is impossible with God."

"I am the Lord's servant," Mary answered. "May it be to me as you have said." Then the angel left her.

At that time Mary got ready and hurried to a town in the hill country of Judea, where she entered Zechariah's home and greeted Elizabeth. When Elizabeth heard Mary's greeting, the baby leaped in her womb, and Elizabeth was filled with the Holy Spirit. In a loud voice she exclaimed, "Blessed are you among women, and blessed is the child you will bear!"

Although uncertain, it's generally thought that Elizabeth and Zechariah lived in the town of Ein Karem, which was about 6 kilometres west of Jerusalem, and it would probably have taken Mary three or four days to have made the 145 kilometre journey from Nazareth.

So between the greeting of the Angel Gabriel and the exclamation of Elizabeth we have the first part of the prayer we call the 'Hail Mary.' The Hail Mary is of course recited in the praying of the Rosary, which the Virgin Mary and Bernadette prayed in unison during the Apparitions.

It's remarkable that the Son of God being born to a virgin was actually prophesied seven hundred years earlier by Isaiah, as was the prophecy of Micah that the Messiah would be born in the insignificant village of Bethlehem, which only had a population of several hundred people.

Isaiah 7:13: Then Isaiah said, "Hear now, you house of David! Is it not enough to try the patience of men? Will you try the patience of my God also? Therefore the Lord himself will give you a sign: The virgin will be with child and will give birth to a son, and will call him Immanuel" (meaning God with us).

As Isaiah said, this sign for mankind would not be given by a prophet, but by Almighty God Himself. And so we can see here the unique position that Mary occupies of all the women who have ever lived - she was completely without sin and therefore able to carry the Christ in her womb.

If we think of Mary at the time the Angel Gabriel approached her, we see an innocent and simple young woman, about the age of Bernadette at the time of the Apparitions. Mary accepted the plan that God had for her and all the trials associated with it, without any hesitation. She submitted wholly to the will of God, just as Bernadette would later do herself.

Mary was present at the crucifixion, and her life shows us the selfless love and dedication that she had as a mother. It's self evident that she knows her son Jesus better than anyone else could ever do, and she also knows how to bring a soul to her son's love and to the joy of everlasting life in heaven, if we will only allow her to do so!

Mary had a difficult life starting from before she even gave birth to Jesus, having to travel all the way from Nazareth to Bethlehem in order to comply with the decree of Caesar Augustus that a population census be taken of the Roman Empire.

When Jesus was eight days old, Mary and Joseph took him to the temple to be circumcised and they were met in the temple courts by a devout Jew named Simeon. He'd been assured that he wouldn't die until he'd seen the Christ of God.

Luke 2:34: Then Simeon blessed them and said to Mary, his mother: "This child is destined to cause the falling and rising of many in Israel, and to be a sign that will be spoken against, so that the thoughts of many hearts will be revealed. And a sword will pierce your own soul too."

Simeon's caution that a sword would pierce her soul was one of the seven dolours (sorrows) that Mary would face, and she would have to worry about the meaning of Simeon's words all her life. Another sorrow was when the Holy family had to flee from the tyrant Herod the Great and live in Egypt for a few years, far away from their families and loved ones. The third sorrow was when Jesus went missing for four days until his distraught parents found him sitting in the temple with the teachers of the Law.

The fourth sorrow was when Mary met her beloved son on his way to Calvary, lacerated from the scourging and struggling to stay on his feet. The fifth was when Our Lady stood near the foot of the cross at Golgotha and watched her son die. Mary's sixth sorrow was to see the centurion Longinus pierce the side of Jesus with a lance and shortly after this, receiving the body of her son into her arms. The last sorrow was to see the body of Jesus being placed in the nearby tomb by Nicodemus and Joseph of Arimathea. These two men were both members of the 69 strong Great Sanhedrin of Jerusalem which had earlier sanctioned the arrest of Jesus, but they were also secret followers of his.

John, the disciple whom Jesus loved, was the only apostle actually present at the crucifixion and Jesus gave this disciple into the care of his mother Mary shortly before his death.

John 19:25: Near the cross of Jesus stood his mother, his mother's sister, Mary the wife of Clopas, and Mary Magdalene. When Jesus saw his mother there, and the disciple whom he loved standing near by, he said to his mother, "Dear woman, here is your son." And to the disciple, "Here is your mother." From that time on, this disciple took her into his home.

The depth of love between mother and son was plain to see at Calvary and the fact that Jesus entrusted Mary to John shows his great concern for her wellbeing. But Jesus surely didn't just give John a spiritual mother in Mary. He also made Mary our mother and indeed the mother of all of God's children!

Entrusting John into Mary's care also shows that Jesus intended for Mary to be involved in the growth of the fledgling Church going forward and we can see her involvement in **Acts1:14**:

'They all joined together constantly in prayer, along with the women and Mary the mother of Jesus, and with his brothers.'

Jesus knew the vital role that John would play as an evangelist and as the author of his gospel and possibly also the Book of Revelation. There was mutual benefit to be derived from Mary helping John and vice versa and they would both need each other's support over the rest of their lives.

No-one knew Jesus quite like Mary and we can only speculate about how often John must have consulted Mary before putting quill to parchment. We'll also never know the wealth of knowledge that Jesus shared with his mother during the thirty years he lived at home before the start of his public ministry.

Reading the account of the Wedding at Cana, it's clear that Mary already knew that Jesus could work miracles and it makes one wonder if he'd performed some miracles before his public ministry had even begun!

There are two traditions in the Church regarding where Mary was assumed into Heaven, with one tradition holding that this was in Jerusalem, but the other placing the event at Ephesus. It's generally accepted that the apostle John died at Selcuk, which is about 3 kilometres from Ephesus.

The tradition that Mary lived in Ephesus was first proposed by Epiphanius, who was the Bishop of Salamis in Cyprus in the fourth century, but the Eastern Orthodox Church also holds that Mary lived in the vicinity of this city.

Proponents of the Ephesus tradition believe that Mary lived on the slopes of the Bulbul Mountain at a site called Meryemana, The Virgin Mary's house. The original building is long gone but another was rebuilt on the site and has been preserved to this day. Interestingly, there's a spring in the garden which many believe has been a source of healing! Mass is held outdoors there in the evenings.

The Emperor Domitian attempted to kill John by having him poisoned and then thrown into a huge cauldron of boiling oil, in front of a packed Colosseum in Rome. The execution attempts failed and he miraculously emerged unhurt from the boiling oil, which apparently resulted in a very large number of conversions to Christianity on that day. This event was described by the ancient historian Tertullian in chapter 36 of his work, 'The prescription against heretics.'

The enraged Domitian then exiled John to the penal island of Patmos, which is where he's believed to have written Revelation. However after his exile, John returned to Ephesus.

The Catholic Church has never formally pronounced on whether Mary died or not, but has always taught that she was assumed into heaven, both body and soul.

At the Council of Chalcedon in 451 AD, the Emperor Marcian asked the Patriarch of Jerusalem to bring the relics of Mary to Constantinople, so that they could be enshrined there. But the Patriarch reported back that there were no relics of Mary in Jerusalem!

He said that Mary had died in the presence of the apostles; but her tomb, when opened later was found empty and so the apostles concluded that the body had been taken up into heaven.

The Church of the Sepulchre of Saint Mary at the foot of the Mount of Olives has a crypt, which many believe was the resting place of Mary until her assumption and that it was this tomb, that when opened was found to be empty.

Over the centuries, various churches have been built and later destroyed on this site, but the crypt has always been left undamaged. Even in 1187, when Saladin destroyed the church that had been built by the Crusaders in 1130, he didn't damage the crypt itself.

The actual site of where Mary is thought by many to have died (as opposed to where she may have been buried) also became a place of pilgrimage. The Benedictine Abbey of the Dormition of Mary stands on this site today and is located on Mount Zion, just outside the old city walls near the Zion gate.

If we will only permit it, Mary will act as a powerful intercessor between us and her son Jesus. While Jesus was alive on earth, he listened to Mary, as is evident from the account of the Miracle at Cana, where Jesus converted between 450 and 690 litres of water into wine.

Notice in John's account how the initial reaction of Jesus was not to get involved in working this miracle at all, but that he was motivated to do so by the plea of his mother. In the same way, we can have full confidence that Mary will take our individual pleas to her son and help them to be answered as well.

John 2:1: 'On the third day a wedding took place at Cana in Galilee. Jesus' mother was there, and Jesus and his disciples had also been invited to the wedding.

When the wine was gone, Jesus' mother said to him, "They have no more wine."

"Dear woman, why do you involve me?" Jesus replied. "My time has not yet come."

Nearby stood six stone water jars, the kind used by the Jews for ceremonial washing, each holding from seventy-five to a hundred and fifteen litres.

Jesus said to the servants, "Fill the jars with water"; so they filled them to the brim.

Then he told them, "Now draw some out and take it to the master of the banquet."

They did so, and the master of the banquet tasted the water that had been turned into wine. He did not realise where it had come from, though the servants who had drawn the water knew.

Then he called the bridegroom aside and said, "Everyone brings out the choice wine first and then the cheaper wine after the guests have had too much to drink; but you have saved the best till now."

This, the first of his miraculous signs, Jesus performed at Cana in Galilee. He thus revealed his glory, and his disciples put their faith in him.'

So it's clear that Our Lady played a unique and essential role in the Son of God becoming incarnate in our world. Her womb was an inviolate sanctuary, protecting the Son of God as he grew inside her, and so Mary is surely also a perfect model of motherhood for our world. The Virgin Mary is also our spiritual mother, and ever since her assumption into Heaven, she's performed an ongoing role as an intercessor for us to her Son. Mary was entrusted with this role as a means of helping countless souls towards a deeper devotion of him and to help them along the path to eternal life.

Chapter 7

A call to repentance

Reading through the accounts of the eighteen apparitions at Lourdes, it's clear to see the Virgin Mary's call for us to repent and to have a conversion of heart. For example, at the sixth Apparition on 21st February, Bernadette could see that Our Lady looked deeply saddened and when she asked her why, Our Lady replied, **"Pray for sinners."**

Later, on 24th February at the eighth Apparition, the Virgin Mary repeated these words slowly, deliberately and with great sadness:

"Repentance, Repentance, Repentance."

It was also during this Apparition that Mary said to Bernadette:

"Pray to God for the conversion of sinners."

And later, at the tenth Apparition on 27th February, Mary said to Bernadette:

"Kiss the ground on behalf of sinners."

In fact, Bernadette was seen to kiss the ground or to bow her head to the ground as she prayed for sinners at several of the apparitions, and she was also observed walking on her knees in front of the grotto. In these appeals by Our Lady, we can see a mother's deep concern for her children, and her desire to bring about a conversion of their hearts.

Now it's clear from Scripture that there are consequences for sin at the level of the individual, but also at the macro level, where God sometimes intervenes directly in order to bring mankind back to the right path. In His dealings with us, it seems that God is remarkably tolerant and willing to forgive, but it's also quite apparent that there are limits to this tolerance. After all, it was sin that caused the integrity of the human condition to be compromised and degraded in the Genesis story of the Fall of Man. We also read in Genesis how Cain was tempted and how he also yielded to sin despite God's warning.

Genesis 4:6: Then the Lord said to Cain, "Why are you angry? Why is your face downcast? If you do what is right, will you not be accepted? But if you do not do what is right, sin is crouching at your door; it desires to have you but you must master it."

Cain had made a gift to God by giving up some of his crops as an offering, but his brother Abel had gone further by giving up some of his flock. God looked with favour at the offering brought by Abel, which then made Cain jealous. God knew the feelings that Cain harboured in his heart and warned him to master them, but he ignored the warning and murdered his brother anyway. Now the moral of this story is that sin is crouching at all of our doors, that we have the capacity to master it, and that we are expected to do so.

At the macro level, man's sinfulness eventually resulted in the virtual decimation of mankind after 150 days of flooding at the time of Noah.

Genesis 6:11: 'Now the earth was corrupt in God's sight and was full of violence. God saw how corrupt the earth had become, for all the people on earth had corrupted their ways. So God said to Noah, "I am going to put an end to all people, for the earth is filled with violence because of them. I am surely going to destroy both them and the earth.'

Similarly during the time of Abraham, God destroyed the major plains cities of Sodom and Gomorrah when sin in these cities had become absolutely rife.

Clearly a contravention of any of the Ten Commandments constitutes a serious sin and it's interesting that the prohibitions contained in the Decalogue are consistent with the laws of natural justice and would actually appeal to our conscience even if we were never taught them. Eight of these are prescriptions not to do things and two are positive instructions – keep holy the Sabbath, and honour thy father and mother. Now the wording of the commandments is of course very brief, but it's clear that each one can be applied to a multitude of different situations.

By the time of Jesus, the Jews had formulated a strict and highly specific set of rules as to what actions were sinful, but Jesus pointed out on a number of occasions that a person could still sin even if he kept to the provisions of the law. Jesus therefore took the teachings on what constituted sin to an altogether new level, and offered a quantum shift in their interpretation!

Jesus himself said, **"Do not think that I have come to abolish the Law or the Prophets; I have not come to abolish them but to fulfill them."**

An example was Jesus challenging the Pharisees and Teachers of the Law over their fixation with ritual cleanliness, as in this account in Mark's Gospel.

Mark 7:20: He went on: "What comes out of a man is what makes him 'unclean'. For from within, out of men's hearts, come evil thoughts, sexual immorality, theft, murder, adultery, greed, malice, deceit, lewdness, envy, slander, arrogance and folly. All these evils come from inside and make a man 'unclean'."

Jesus said this privately to his disciples, but it followed on from a discussion with the Pharisees who'd complained to Jesus that his disciples didn't wash their hands before eating. As he often did, Jesus was taking the emphasis away from ceremonies to true spirituality. Here Jesus was saying that you could satisfy the law by washing your hands, lower arms and your pots perfectly, but still be unclean in God's eyes because of your thoughts! He specified thirteen examples of the precursors of sin, which always start in the mind before the physical act is committed.

Jesus also taught that we can sin just as easily by the things that we say as by the things that we do.

Matthew 12:34: "For out of the overflow of the heart the mouth speaks. The good man brings good things out of the good stored up in him, and the evil man brings evil things out of the evil stored up in him. But I tell you that men will have to give account on the Day of Judgment for every careless word they have spoken. For by your words you will be acquitted, and by your words you will be condemned."

During his ministry, a rich young man once approached Jesus and asked him what he had to do in order to inherit eternal life. In his reply Jesus reiterated the importance of keeping the Ten Commandments, but he also implied that a lack of charity and an attachment to wealth was a serious sin too.

Mark 10:17: As Jesus started on his way, a man ran up to him and fell on his knees before him. "Good teacher," he asked, "what must I do to inherit eternal life?"

"Why do you call me good?" Jesus answered. "No one is good – except God alone. You know the commandments: 'Do not murder, do not commit adultery, do not steal, do not give false testimony, do not defraud, honour your father and mother.'"

"Teacher," he declared, "all these I have kept since I was a boy."

Jesus looked at him and loved him. "One thing you lack," he said. "Go, sell everything you have and give to the poor, and you will have treasure in heaven. Then come, follow me."

At this the man's face fell. He went away sad, because he had great wealth. Jesus looked around and said to his disciples, "How hard it is for the rich to enter the kingdom of God!"

Another example of Jesus taking the teachings on sin to a whole new level was when he spoke on the subject of adultery.

Matthew 5:27: "You have heard that it was said, 'Do not commit adultery.' But I tell you that anyone who looks at a woman lustfully has already committed adultery with her in his heart. If your right eye causes you to sin, gouge it out and throw it away. It is better for you to lose one part of your body than for your whole body to be thrown into hell. And if your right hand causes you to sin, cut it off and throw it away. It is better for you to lose one part of your body than for your whole body to go into hell."

So regarding the commandment 'Thou shall not commit adultery,' Jesus was reminding the Jews that it wasn't just the physical act that was sinful, but that we could also sin by our thoughts.

Jesus also told the parable of 'The rich man and Lazarus' to show us that if we neglect the people who are suffering around us, then we're also committing a serious sin. In other words, we can sin not just by the things that we do, but by withholding charity, mercy, and love.

Luke 16:19: "There was a rich man who was dressed in purple and fine linen and lived in luxury every day. At his gate was laid a beggar named Lazarus, covered with sores and longing to eat what fell from the rich man's table. Even the dogs came and licked his sores. The time came when the beggar died and the angels carried him to Abraham's side. The rich man also died and was buried.

"In Hell, where he was in torment, he looked up and saw Abraham far away, with Lazarus by his side. So he called to him, 'Father Abraham, have pity on me and send Lazarus to dip the tip of his finger in water and cool my tongue, because I am in agony in this fire.'

"But Abraham replied, 'Son, remember that in your lifetime you received your good things, while Lazarus received bad things, but now he is comforted here and you are in agony. And besides all this, between us and you a great chasm has been fixed, so that those who want to go from here to you cannot, nor can anyone cross over from there to us.'

"He answered, 'Then I beg you, father, send Lazarus to my father's house, for I have five brothers. Let him warn them, so that they will not also come to this place of torment.'

"Abraham replied, 'They have Moses and the Prophets; let them listen to them.'

"'No, father Abraham,' he said, 'but if someone from the dead goes to them, they will repent.'

"He said to him, 'If they do not listen to Moses and the Prophets, they will not be convinced even if someone rises from the dead.'"

In this parable, the rich man hadn't actually done anything to harm Lazarus, but he was still sent to Hell for having ignored his suffering. The rich man became fully aware of the need for repentance when he was in Hell, but by then it was too late as he'd been judged and his state was fixed for all eternity.

So instead he focused on getting his family to repent and he asked Abraham to send Lazarus to his father's house to warn his brothers of the need to change. This shows that the Rich Man wasn't all bad, as he at least had genuine concern for his own family, which is one of the frightening aspects of the story.

The parable above dovetails nicely with the teaching of Jesus about the final judgement and how the sheep will be separated from the goats.

Again the message is that neglect of people who are in need is sinful, and Jesus calls on us to be proactive and to show compassion, as in the Parable of the Good Samaritan.

Matthew 25:41: "Then he will say to those on his left, 'Depart from me, you who are cursed, into the eternal fire prepared for the devil and his angels. For I was hungry and you gave me nothing to eat, I was thirsty and you gave me nothing to drink, I was a stranger and you did not invite me in, I needed clothes and you did not clothe me, I was sick and in prison and you did not look after me.'

"They also will answer, 'Lord, when did we see you hungry or thirsty or a stranger or needing clothes or sick or in prison, and did not help you?'

"He will reply, 'Truly I tell you, whatever you did not do for one of the least of these, you did not do for me.'

"Then they will go away to eternal punishment, but the righteous to eternal life."

Now the Church rightly makes a distinction between venial or less serious sins and mortal sins, which are contraventions of the Ten Commandments. However all sins can be forgiven if a person repents and confesses them, with the exception of blasphemy against the Holy Spirit, and this is because if a person dies in a state of denial of the very existence of God, there can clearly be no forgiveness.

Matthew 12:31: "And so I tell you, every sin and blasphemy will be forgiven men, but the blasphemy against the Spirit will not be forgiven. Anyone who speaks a word against the Son of Man will be forgiven, but anyone who speaks against the Holy Spirit will not be forgiven, either in this age or in the age to come."

Here Jesus is saying that there's no grey area when it comes to belief in him and that everyone has a choice to either reject or to accept him as the Son of God. If a person rejects Jesus in their life, then they're not a party to the new covenant, and so they cannot receive the sanctifying grace of his sacrifice on the cross. From this we can see that **atheism** has become one of the major sins in our modern world, and as Mary requested at Lourdes, we all need to pray for the conversion of souls.

Another great sin of modern times is that of **abortion**, and the number of abortions being carried out today is simply staggering. For example, it's estimated that there were 43.8 million abortions in 2008 alone. The worldwide abortion rate in that year was 28 abortions per 1000 women of child bearing age (15 to 44 years). So this means that almost 3% of women of child bearing age in the world had an abortion in that year.

Abortion has been recognised as a very serious sin since the time of the early Church and Tertullian, one of the Fathers of the Church, described it in his work, the Apologeticum, which was written around 197 AD (verse 8, chapter 9):

"In our case, a murder being once for all forbidden, we may not destroy even the fetus in the womb, while as yet the human being derives blood from the other parts of the body for its sustenance. To hinder a birth is merely a speedier man-killing; nor does it matter whether you take away a life that is born, or destroy one that is coming to birth. That is a man which is going to be one; you have the fruit already in its seed."

Pope John Paul II released the encyclical '**Evangelium Vitae**' on the 25th of March 1995 concerning the inviolability of human life, and it specifically covered murder, abortion and euthanasia. One of the declarations from the Pope's encyclical was:

Evangelium Vitae 58: Among all the crimes which can be committed against life, procured abortion has characteristics making it particularly serious and deplorable. The Second Vatican Council defines abortion, together with infanticide, as an 'unspeakable crime.'

Unfortunately our world seems to have become completely numb to the sin of abortion, and the words of Pope Pius XII come to mind. In a radio address on the 26th of October 1946 to the U.S. National Catechetical Congress in Boston, Pope Pius XII said:

'The sin of the century is the loss of the sense of sin.'

These stark words were later quoted by John Paul II at the Synod of Bishops in October 1983.

Other sins that have become far more prominent in modern times include pornography and paedophilia.

Now God's laws are immutable and so they need to be the benchmark by which our actions are deemed sinful or not. It's easy for us to forget that God's definition of what constitutes a sin is timeless, unlike man's laws which constantly evolve and redefine what actions are legal and which are not. At no time in history has there been such a great gulf between the two and we now have protected in law actions which are clearly contrary to God's laws, such as abortion.

At Lourdes, Mary was clearly concerned about sinners and she called on us to repent, as she knows that this is necessary for us to secure eternal life as individuals, and for us to have peace in our world at the macro level.

Naturally, Man has never found the idea of having to repent for his sins easy to accept, even before the death and resurrection of Jesus. This is because it takes us out of our comfort zones and makes us admit that we aren't perfect after all, and that we do have failings – failings which have compromised our relationship with God. But we should rather focus on the **sanctifying grace** that comes through the Sacrament of Confession, which removes all the guilt of sin and which draws us ever closer to God's love.

Unfortunately there's a popular misconception that it's no longer necessary for us to repent because Jesus has already atoned for all of our sins anyway. But he himself said **after his resurrection** that we still need to confess our sins!

John 20:19: On the evening of that first day of the week, when the disciples were together, with the doors locked for fear of the Jews, Jesus came and stood among them and said, "Peace be with you!"

After he said this, he showed them his hands and side. The disciples were overjoyed when they saw the Lord. Again Jesus said, "Peace be with you! As the Father has sent me, I am sending you."

And with that he breathed on them and said, "Receive the Holy Spirit. If you forgive anyone his sins, they are forgiven; if you do not forgive them, they are not forgiven."

So it's crystal clear from this reading that Jesus empowered his apostles to forgive sins, just as he'd done himself throughout his public ministry. Despite this, some people question whether this delegation of responsibility to forgive sins was for the Apostles only, or if it was passed on to others when they received the Holy Spirit by the laying on of hands by the Apostles. This issue was addressed at the Council of Trent in 1551 AD where the following proclamation was made:

"The Lord instituted the Sacrament of Penance principally when after his resurrection he breathed upon his disciples and said: 'Receive the Holy Spirit. If you forgive the sins of any, they are forgiven; if you retain the sins of any, they are retained.' The universal consensus of the Fathers has always acknowledged that by so sublime an action and such clear words the power of forgiving and retaining sins was given to the apostles and their lawful successors for reconciling the faithful who have fallen away after baptism."

The lawful successors are clearly ordained priests.

But just how far back in Church history can we trace the practice of confessing sins? Well, one of the proclamations of the 4th Lateran Council of 1215 AD was: "All the faithful should individually confess all their sins in a faithful manner to their own priest at least once a year."

But there's evidence that it was common practice for Christians to attend confession from long before this. For example in 459 AD, Pope Leo I wrote a letter to his bishops under the title 'Magna Indignatione' in which he discussed confession. The pope wrote:

"With regard to penance, what is demanded of the faithful is clearly not that an acknowledgement of the nature of individual sins written in a little book be read publicly, since it suffices that the states of consciences be made known to the priests alone in secret confession."

Going further back, we have a reference to confession in chapter 4 of the Didache, which is generally dated to the end of the first century AD. This brief treatise, also known as The Teaching of the Twelve Apostles, is the oldest written catechism ever found and it covers Christian ethics as well as Baptism and the Eucharist.

"In the church you shall acknowledge your transgressions, and you shall not come near for your prayer with an evil conscience."

But if we want evidence that repentance was actively encouraged by the apostles themselves after the resurrection, we just need to look at the book of Acts.

Acts 2:38: Peter replied, "Repent and be baptised, every one of you, in the name of Jesus Christ for the forgiveness of your sins. And you will receive the gift of the Holy Spirit.

Acts 3:19: Repent, then, and turn to God, so that your sins may be wiped out, that times of refreshing may come from the Lord, and that he may send the Christ, who has been appointed for you – even Jesus.

So it's clear that the practice of confessing one's sins goes right back to the earliest beginnings of the Church. Confessions would have been made in public initially, which would have been highly embarrassing, and so over time it evolved into the private confession we know today.

It's important for us to remember that it's not the priests who are doing the forgiving, but that they're acting 'in persona Christi' and that the grace of God's forgiveness is just being channeled through them. This is why priests use these specific words at confession: 'By the power given me by Almighty God, I absolve you of your sins in the name of the Father and of the Son and of the Holy Spirit.'

An example of the forgiveness that comes with repentance at the macro level can be found in the biblical account of Nineveh. God was angered by the sinfulness that was prevalent in this great city and so he sent the reluctant prophet Jonah to warn the people of its impending destruction.

Jonah 3:4: On the first day, Jonah started into the city. He proclaimed: "Forty more days and Nineveh will be overturned."

The Ninevites believed God. They declared a fast, and all of them, from the greatest to the least, put on sackcloth. When the news reached the king of Nineveh, he rose from his throne, took off his royal robes, covered himself with sackcloth and sat down in the dust. Then he issued a proclamation in Nineveh:

"By the decree of the king and his nobles: Do not let any man or beast, herd or flock, taste anything; do not let them eat or drink. But let man and beast be covered with sackcloth. Let everyone

call urgently on God. Let them give up their evil ways and their violence.

"Who knows? God may yet relent and with compassion turn from his fierce anger so that we will not perish." When God saw what they did and how they turned from their evil ways, he had compassion and did not bring upon them the destruction he had threatened."

The lesson of Nineveh is that the punishment that's due for sin can be put aside by God if we genuinely repent.

In the gospels we read of John the Baptist calling people to repent through a ceremonial baptism in the river Jordan. John was the last of the Old Testament prophets and the first of the prophets of the New Testament and he wanted people to repent in order to be in a fit spiritual state so that they could accept the teachings of Christ.

Matthew 3:1: 'In those days John the Baptist came preaching in the Desert of Judea and saying, "Repent, for the kingdom of heaven is near." This is he who was spoken of through the prophet Isaiah: "A voice of one calling in the desert, 'Prepare the way for the Lord, make straight paths for him.'"

John's clothes were made of camel's hair, and he had a leather belt around his waist. His food was locusts and wild honey. People went out to him from Jerusalem and all Judea and the whole region of the Jordan. Confessing their sins, they were baptised by him in the Jordan River.'

What's interesting is that Jesus himself made this baptism of repentance even though he was clearly without sin, and he surely did this as an example for all of us to follow.

Matthew 3:13: Then Jesus came from Galilee to the Jordan to be baptised by John. But John tried to deter him, saying, "I need to be baptised by you, and do you come to me?"

Jesus replied, "Let it be so now; it is proper for us to do this to fulfill all righteousness."

Then John consented. As soon as Jesus was baptised, he went up out of the water. At that moment heaven was opened, and he saw the Spirit of God descending like a dove and lighting on him.

And a voice from heaven said, "This is my Son, whom I love; with him I am well pleased."

It's fascinating that the voice of God was heard on this occasion and it was the first of three situations when God was heard speaking. The other two occasions were at the transfiguration (Matthew 17:5), and also just after the triumphal entry of Jesus into Jerusalem, just days before his death (John 12:28).

Jesus often spoke about the need for repentance during his public ministry and an example of this was when he was asked what he thought about the execution of some Galilean men by the Roman Governor, Pontius Pilate.

Luke 13:1: Now there were some present at that time who told Jesus about the Galileans whose blood Pilate had mixed with their sacrifices. Jesus answered, "Do you think that these Galileans were worse sinners than all the other Galileans because they suffered this way? I tell you, no! But unless you repent, you too will all perish. Or those eighteen who died when the tower in Siloam fell on them – do you think they were more guilty than all the others living in Jerusalem? I tell you, no! But unless you repent, you too will all perish."

In Matthew's Gospel there's another example of Jesus warning the Pharisees about the need for them to repent.

Matthew 21:31: Jesus said to them, "I tell you the truth, the tax collectors and the prostitutes are entering the kingdom of God ahead of you. For John came to you to show you the way to righteousness, and you did not believe him, but the tax collectors and the prostitutes did. And even after you saw this, you did not repent and believe him."

At other times, Jesus described the joy that there is in heaven when a sinful person repents and turns away from sin, such as in his parables about the lost sheep and the lost coin.

Luke 15:3: Then Jesus told them this parable: "Suppose one of you has a hundred sheep and loses one of them. Does he not leave the ninety-nine in the open country and go after the lost sheep until he finds it? And when he finds it, he joyfully puts it on his shoulders and goes home. Then he calls his friends and

neighbours together and says, 'Rejoice with me; I have found my lost sheep.'

"I tell you that in the same way there will be more rejoicing in heaven over one sinner who repents than over ninety-nine righteous persons who do not need to repent.

"Or suppose a woman has ten silver coins and loses one. Does she not light a lamp, sweep the house and search carefully until she finds it? And when she finds it, she calls her friends and neighbours together and says, 'Rejoice with me; I have found my lost coin.' In the same way, I tell you, there is rejoicing in the presence of the angels of God over one sinner who repents."

Here Jesus shows us the unlimited love that God has for His creation and His desire for all of us to be saved, but again the starting point has to be repentance.

The same theme is found in the Parable of the Prodigal Son, where the father looked out over the fields every single day, hoping that his son would one day return to his love. When the son came to his senses and asked for forgiveness, the father showed a wonderful outpouring of love and restored him in every way possible.

A wonderful example of the compassion that Jesus will show us as individuals if we repent is found in Luke's Gospel, where a sinful woman put her shame and embarrassment aside to come to Jesus for forgiveness, without uttering a single word.

Luke 7:36: 'Now one of the Pharisees invited Jesus to have dinner with him, so he went to the Pharisee's house and reclined at the table. When a woman who had lived a sinful life in that town learned that Jesus was eating at the Pharisee's house, she brought an alabaster jar of perfume, and as she stood behind him at his feet weeping, she began to wet his feet with her tears. Then she wiped them with her hair, kissed them and poured perfume on them.

When the Pharisee who had invited him saw this, he said to himself, "If this man were a prophet, he would know who is touching him and what kind of woman she is, that she is a sinner."

Jesus answered him, "Simon, I have something to tell you."

"Tell me, teacher," he said.

"Two men owed money to a certain money-lender. One owed him five hundred denarii, and the other fifty. Neither of them had the money to pay him back, so he cancelled the debts of both. Now which of them will love him more?"

Simon replied, "I suppose the one who had the bigger debt cancelled."

"You have judged correctly," Jesus said.

Then he turned towards the woman and said to Simon, "Do you see this woman? I came to your house. You did not give me any water for my feet, but she wet my feet with her tears and wiped them with her hair. You did not give me a kiss, but this woman, from the time I entered, has not stopped kissing my feet. You did not put oil on my head, but she has poured perfume on my feet. Therefore, I tell you, her many sins have been forgiven, for she loved much. But he who has been forgiven little loves little."

Then Jesus said to her, "Your sins are forgiven.'"

But perhaps we can take the greatest lesson on this subject from the final moments of Christ's life, as he hung on the cross at Calvary.

Luke 23:39: One of the criminals who hung there hurled insults at him: "Aren't you the Christ? Save yourself and us!"

But the other criminal rebuked him. "Don't you fear God," he said, "since you are under the same sentence? We are punished justly, for we are getting what our deeds deserve. But this man has done nothing wrong."

Then he said, "Jesus, remember me when you come into your kingdom."

Jesus answered him, "I tell you the truth, today you will be with me in paradise."

So Dismas, the good thief, repented at the very end of his life and made the perfect confession. He acknowledged his sins and recognised the need for forgiveness, unlike the other thief, Gestas. Dismas joined his sufferings to that of Jesus hanging on the cross right next to him and was forgiven at that very moment. This gives us all hope and it shows us that it's never too late to repent and to turn to God.

But the response of Dismas and Gestas is also a lesson in how we should approach human suffering and terminal disease. The two men were experiencing exactly the same pain and yet their response to it could not have been more different.

Gestas was full of anger, blaming and insulting Jesus and refusing to accept that he was going to die or that he had any need to ask for forgiveness, and as a result he denied himself the opportunity of going to heaven.

Dismas on the other hand, didn't allow his pain to make him bitter and angry with God, but rather he channeled his suffering into something positive by turning to Jesus. For this he received the greatest reward possible, which is eternal life.

At Lourdes, Our Lady made a plea for us to repent, echoing what her son Jesus had said so often during his earthly life, and Mary's role in drawing souls to penance and to the love of God has always been recognised by the Church.

At the month long Synod of Bishops held in October 1983, John Paul II reiterated that penance was closely connected with reconciliation to God.

Regarding the vital role of Our Lady he said the following:

'The first means of this salvific action is that of prayer. It is certain that the Blessed Virgin, mother of Christ and of the church, and the saints, who have now reached the end of their earthly journey and possess God's glory, sustain by their intercession their brethren who are on pilgrimage through the world, in the commitment to conversion, to faith, to getting up again after every fall, to acting in order to help the growth of communion and peace in the church and in the world.'

Chapter 8

The Lourdes - Fatima link

Reading the accounts of the apparitions at Lourdes and Fatima it's clear that there are consistent themes running through both events. Unfortunately there's been a tendency to view each of these in isolation, but by doing so we're in danger of not seeing the commonality between the two. The key message from Lourdes and from Fatima, separated by just 59 years of history, is remarkably similar, and the two events complement and reinforce each other very well.

The single greatest revelation at Lourdes was clearly Our Lady declaring, "**I am the Immaculate Conception**" at the 16th apparition on 25th March 1858.

At Fatima, the greatest revelations were made at the third apparition on 13th July 1917, when Mary gave Lucia, Francisco and Jacinta a frightening **vision of hell**.

On this day she also made a plea for mankind to stop offending God by its sins, and she warned that a war worse than World War I would break out unless this happened. But the Virgin Mary told the children that the chastisement of war could be prevented, saying that she would later return in order to ask for the **Consecration of Russia to Her Immaculate Heart**.

Mary also said that when she returned she would ask for a devotion, the **Communion of Reparation on the First Five Saturdays**, to be adopted by the faithful. She said that if people ceased offending God through sin and that if these two specific requests were adopted, then the world would indeed have peace.

Now this is how Lucia dos Santos described the vision of hell:

"The rays of light seemed to penetrate the earth, and we saw, as it were a sea of fire. Plunged in this fire were demons and souls in human form, like transparent burning embers, all blackened or burnished bronze, floating about in the conflagration, now raised into the air by the flames that issued from within themselves together with great clouds of smoke, now falling back on every

side like sparks in huge fires, without weight or equilibrium, amid shrieks and groans of pain and despair, which horrified us and made us tremble with fear. The demons could be distinguished by their terrifying and repellent likeness to frightful and unknown animals, black and transparent like burning coals."

After giving the children this vision, Mary said:

"You have seen hell where the souls of poor sinners go. To save them, God wishes to establish in the world devotion to my Immaculate Heart. If what I say to you is done, many souls will be saved and there will be peace.

"The war is going to end; but if people do not cease offending God, a worse one will break out during the pontificate of Pius XI. When you see a night illumined by an unknown light, know that this is the great sign given you by God that He is about to punish the world for its crimes, by means of war, famine and persecutions of the Church and of the Holy Father.

"To prevent this, I shall come to ask for the consecration of Russia to my Immaculate Heart, and the Communion of Reparation on the First Saturdays. If my requests are heeded, Russia will be converted, and there will be peace; if not, she will spread her errors throughout the world, causing wars and persecutions of the Church. The good will be martyred, the Holy Father will have much to suffer, various nations will be annihilated.

"In the end, my Immaculate Heart will triumph. The Holy Father will consecrate Russia to me, and she will be converted, and a period of peace will be granted to the world. In Portugal, the dogma of the faith will always be preserved .."

But the children were also given another revelation on 13th July 1917 which came to be known as **the third secret**, and which would later cause massive controversy. Lucia wrote this vision down in a letter addressed to Bishop da Silva, the Bishop of Leiria Fatima in January 1944, but the Vatican only made it public on 26th June 2000.

"I write in obedience to you, my God, who command me to do so through his Excellency the Bishop of Leiria and through your Most Holy Mother and mine.

"After the two parts which I have already explained, at the left of Our Lady and a little above, we saw an Angel with a flaming sword in his left hand; flashing, it gave out flames that looked as though they would set the world on fire; but they died out in contact with the splendour that Our Lady radiated towards him from her right hand: pointing to the earth with his right hand, the Angel cried out in a loud voice: "Penance, Penance, Penance!"

"And we saw in an immense light that is God: 'something similar to how people appear in a mirror when they pass in front of it' a Bishop dressed in White 'we had the impression that it was the Holy Father'. Other Bishops, Priests, men and women Religious going up a steep mountain, at the top of which there was a big Cross of rough-hewn trunks as of a cork-tree with the bark; before reaching there the Holy Father passed through a big city half in ruins and half trembling with halting step, afflicted with pain and sorrow, he prayed for the souls of the corpses he met on his way; having reached the top of the mountain, on his knees at the foot of the big Cross he was killed by a group of soldiers who fired bullets and arrows at him, and in the same way there died one after another the other Bishops, Priests, men and women Religious, and various lay people of different ranks and positions. Beneath the two arms of the Cross there were two Angels each with a crystal aspersorium in his hand, in which they gathered up the blood of the Martyrs and with it sprinkled the souls that were making their way to God."

Now what's remarkable is that Mary's warning about the consequences of sin causing war and of Russia spreading her errors throughout the world, was given in July 1917, which was three months **before** the start of the Russian Civil War, which broke out in October of that year.

Russia had been on the side of the Allies in World War I and at the time Mary made this revelation, that country didn't pose a threat to the Allied nations in any way. However, the Civil War would end in October 1922 with victory for the Bolshevics, and Russia would then become a communist state.

Our Lady, with the child Jesus, subsequently appeared to Lucia on 10th December 1925 when she was in the Dorothean Convent near

Pontevedra in Spain, to give her specific details about the First Five Saturday's devotion. On this occasion Mary said:

"Look, my daughter, at my Heart, surrounded with thorns with which ungrateful men pierce me at every moment by their blasphemies and ingratitude. You can at least try to console me and say that I promise to assist at the hour of death, with the graces necessary for salvation, all those who, for five consecutive months, shall confess, receive Holy Communion, recite five decades of the Rosary, and keep me company for fifteen minutes while meditating on the fifteen mysteries of the Rosary, with the intention of making reparation to me."

Mary's assurance that she will give anyone who makes this devotion the graces necessary for their salvation, is surely the most wonderful and reassuring of all promises!

Jesus again appeared to Lucia in the garden of the Dorothean Convent in Pontevedra on 15th February 1926 to ask that this devotion be adopted.

Then three years later on 13th June 1929, the Virgin Mary again appeared to Lucia when she was at the Dorothean Novitiate near Tuy to ask for the consecration of Russia to Her Immaculate Heart, but unfortunately the Church was very slow to respond to this request.

The vision of hell was published by the Vatican on the 25th anniversary of the first apparition, the 13th of May 1942, in the middle of World War II.

However, it was only after the assassination attempt on Pope John Paul II on 13th May 1981, the anniversary of the first apparition that he decided to consecrate Russia to the Immaculate Heart of Mary. The pope was utterly convinced that Mary had directly intervened to prevent him being killed by the bullets from Mehmet Ali Agca's gun. So the Vatican finally decided to release the text of the third secret on 26th June 2000, which was about 83 years after Lucia had been given the vision.

At both Lourdes and Fatima, Mary appeared to innocent, simple young people. At the time of the apparitions in Lourdes, Bernadette was 14, and at Fatima, Lucia dos Santos was 10, Francisco Marto was 9, and Jacinta Marto was just 7 years of age.

This is reminiscent of what Jesus said during his ministry about the mysteries of faith being revealed to the poor and uneducated people.

Matthew 11:25: At that time Jesus said, "I praise you, Father, Lord of heaven and earth, because you have hidden these things from the wise and learned, and revealed them to little children. Yes, Father, for this was your good pleasure."

In both cases Mary appeared at a time of poverty and disease, and at the time of the apparitions at Fatima, Europe was also afflicted by the horror of World War I. She came to give hope and encouragement and to draw people back to the love of God.

None of the apparitions were in the children's homes, but rather they were outside in remote places, and at both Lourdes and Fatima it was only the children who could see and communicate with Mary.

Perhaps it was to be expected, but at Fatima and at Lourdes there was widespread scepticism and hostility shown towards the visionaries, and yet the children somehow remained resolute throughout their questioning and abuse.

At Lourdes, life was made difficult for Bernadette by people in authority such as Jacques Vital Dutour, the Public Prosecutor; Dominique Jacomet, the Police Commissioner, Jean Baptiste Estrade from the tax office, and Judge Clement Ribes.

At Fatima the same was true, and Artur de Oliveira Santos, the Mayor of Ourem which had jurisdiction over Fatima, even abducted the children and imprisoned them overnight, during which time all sorts of threats were made against them, including to have them boiled alive.

The Church endorsed the authenticity of the apparitions at Lourdes three and a half years after they happened, when Bishop Laurence, the Bishop of Nevers, declared that the faithful were justified in believing the apparitions with certainty.

However the Church took far longer to recognise the events at Fatima, with Bishop da Silva, the Bishop of Leiria-Fatima, only declaring the apparitions to be worthy of belief on 13th October 1930, which was the 13th anniversary of the Miracle of the Sun.

At both Lourdes and Fatima Our Lady asked for a chapel to be built. In fact at Lourdes she asked for this on 18th February and again at the

2nd and 3rd of March apparitions. The construction of chapels, and later churches and Basilica's in both towns has provided a lasting legacy, with tens of millions of pilgrims having visited these sites.

Another common theme was that Bernadette, Jacinta and Francisco all suffered greatly, and yet all three accepted this without any complaint. In fact they proactively used their pain to achieve a positive effect. By accepting their trials and by uniting them with Jesus through prayer, **they offered their suffering up as a sacrifice to God**.

Now it's been accepted from the time of the Patriarchs that great value can come out of the sacrifice of the innocent, hence the practice of offering up lambs or other young animals as burnt offerings. The ultimate example of this is of course Jesus, who was completely innocent, offering himself up on the cross, and the redemptive power that comes from this sacrifice is infinite.

Bernadette suffered from the effects of having contracted cholera as a child, and she had very bad asthma and later tuberculosis, dying at the age of 35. Jacinta contracted the Spanish Flu and then developed tuberculosis, passing away when she was just 9 years of age. Francisco also contracted the Spanish Flu, suffering from its effects for several months before dying at the age of 10.

It's a sobering statistic that the Spanish Flu pandemic of January 1918 to December 1920 killed at least 50 million people, which was about 3% of the world's population at that time.

An example of how the children were able to channel their illness into something positive is clear from what Francisco said when he was asked how much he was suffering shortly before he died.

He replied: "Quite a lot, but never mind! I am suffering to console Our Lord, and afterwards, within a short time, I am going to Heaven!"

When Jacinta was seriously ill, she said to her cousin Lucia:

"It will not be long now before I go to Heaven. You will remain here to make known that God wishes to establish in the world **devotion to the Immaculate Heart of Mary**.

"When you are to say this, don't go and hide. Tell everybody that God grants us graces through the Immaculate heart of Mary; that people are to ask her for them; and that the Heart of Jesus wants the Immaculate

Heart of Mary to be venerated at His side. Tell them also to pray to the Immaculate Heart of Mary for peace since God has entrusted it to her.

"If I could only put into the hearts of all, the fire that is burning within my own heart, and that makes me love the Hearts of Jesus and Mary so very much!"

It's astonishing that a nine year old could describe the Virgin Mary's role in bringing peace to our world and in helping us along the path to salvation with such clarity, but these truths were of course revealed to her during the apparitions.

Jacinta often said to Lucia that she was offering her sufferings for the **conversion of sinners** and she would kiss her crucifix and say, "O my Jesus! I love You, and I want to suffer very much for love of You. O Jesus! Now you can convert many sinners, because this is really a big sacrifice!"

Like Bernadette, Lucia dos Santos became a nun, but unlike her she lived a very long life and passed away at the age of 97 on 13th February 2005. Jacinta was quite correct about the role that Lucia would play in drawing the attention of the Church and the world to the requests made by Our Lady at Fatima.

Lucia tirelessly pleaded with successive popes to action the requests that Our Lady had made known to her, including the consecration of Russia to Her Immaculate Heart, and the First Five Saturdays devotion.

Another common feature of Lourdes and Fatima is that Bernadette Soubirous and Jacinta Marto remained incorrupt after death. The **incorrupt bodies of the saints** are clearly miracles given to us by God as evidence of the sanctity of these remarkable people.

In the case of Bernadette, her body was still incorrupt at the final exhumation on 18th April 1925, which was 46 years after her death, and Doctor Comte who undertook the examination was shocked that the liver was completely undecayed after this length of time. He said that when he cut into it, the liver looked almost normal i.e. like the liver of a living person, and that this was not a natural phenomenon.

Similarly when Jacinta's coffin was opened on 1st May 1951, which was 31 years after she died, her face was still completely incorrupt and undecayed.

But both Lourdes and Fatima are associated with other supernatural phenomena and these are **miraculous healings** and also **miracles involving nature**.

Many believe that the spring at Massabielle is in itself a miracle, as there was no spring at the site at all before Bernadette scratched at the ground there. The water flows at up to 40 litres per minute, or 57600 litres a day.

The water from the spring has been associated with thousands of cures, although only 70 have been officially recognised by the Church thus far. The instantaneous healings of people suffering from untreatable life-threatening diseases cannot be explained by doctors or by scientists. When you read through the individual accounts of these healings you're left stunned, but also comforted that the miraculous power of Almighty God is at work in our world right now!

You feel the same emotions at other sites where there's been a history of miraculous cures up to the present day, such as in the Basilica of the Blessed Virgin of Ta Pinu on the Maltese island of Gozo, where the walls are covered with hundreds of testimonies of miraculous healings.

Our Lady first appeared at the Cova da Iria in Fatima on 13th May 1917, and on that first visit she asked the children to come every month on the 13th day of the month, for six consecutive months.

On 13th July she said that she would work a miracle in the month of October 'for all to see and believe.' Now Our Lady repeated that same statement in both the August and September apparitions as well.

It was on 13th October 1917 that the greatest miracle in modern history, the **Miracle of the Sun** was witnessed by a crowd estimated at 70,000 gathered at the Cova da Iria.

Believers, atheists, scientists, religious and lay people in the crowd were all left stunned at the site of the sun performing a dazzling array of movements which were physically impossible in terms of physics and astronomy.

Doctor Almeida Garrett, who was Professor of the Faculty of Science at the University of Coimbra wrote an account of the phenomenon that he witnessed that day, and a brief part of it is given below.

"Then, suddenly, one heard a clamor, a cry of anguish breaking from all the people. The sun, whirling wildly, seemed all at once to loosen itself from the firmament and, blood red, advance threateningly upon the earth as if to crush us with its huge and fiery weight. The sensation during those moments was truly terrible.

"All the phenomena which I have described were observed by me in a calm and serene state of mind without any emotional disturbance. It is for others to interpret and explain them. Finally, I must declare that never, before or after October 13 (1917), have I observed similar atmospheric or solar phenomena."

Doctor Domingos Pinto Coelho also witnessed the astonishing event that day and wrote an article about it for the Ordem newspaper:

"The sun, at one moment surrounded with scarlet flame, at another aureoled in yellow and deep purple, seemed to be in an exceedingly swift and whirling movement, at times appearing to be loosened from the sky and to be approaching the earth, strongly radiating heat."

The Reverend Joaquin Laurenco also described what he saw that day, when he was a boy living in Alburitel, eighteen kilometres from Fatima:

"I feel incapable of describing what I saw. I looked fixedly at the sun, which seemed pale and did not hurt my eyes. Looking like a ball of snow, revolving on itself, it suddenly seemed to come down in a zig-zag, menacing the earth. Terrified, I ran and hid myself among the people, who were weeping and expecting the end of the world at any moment."

Alfredo de Silva Santos was also present at the Cova da Iria that day and he wrote:

"When Lucia called out, 'Look at the sun!' the whole multitude echoed, 'Look at the sun!' It was a day of incessant drizzle but a few moments before the miracle it left off raining. I can hardly find words to describe what followed.

"The sun began to move and at a certain moment appeared to be detached from the sky and about to hurtle on us like a wheel of flame. My wife – we had been married only a short time – fainted. I fell on my knees oblivious of everything and when I got up I don't know what I said. I think I began to cry out like the others."

But the Miracle of the Sun at Fatima on 13th October 1917 wasn't the only miracle associated with the apparitions there.

On 13th July of that year, Our Lady explained to the children that the sins of mankind were greatly offending God and that unless they ceased doing so, then a war worse than World War I would break out during the pontificate of Pope Pius XI. Our Lady's specific words were:

"When you see a **night illumined by an unknown light**, know that this is the great sign given you by God that He is about to punish the world for its crimes, by means of war, famine and persecutions of the Church and of the Holy Father."

What's incredible is that Ambrogio Achille Ratti, the man who would go on to become Pope on 6th February 1922 and who would choose the name Pius XI, was at the time of the Fatima Apparitions just a priest and the prefect of the Vatican Library!

On the **25th of January 1938**, during the pontificate of Pope Pius XI, the night sky was illumined by what scientists called the most spectacular Aurora Borealis event in recorded history. It was witnessed throughout the whole of Europe and was detected by astronomical observatories throughout the continent.

This Aurora Borealis was differentiated from others by just how far south it extended and it was seen clearly in Sicily, in Gibraltar and even in Madeira. It was also visible in Bermuda and as far south as San Diego in Southern California.

Fire brigades were called out in Austria and Switzerland to attend to suspected fires, because the sky appeared as a huge flaming red curtain. Along the Pyrenees, the Aurora caused panic as people thought that the sky was ablaze as a result of an aerial bombardment in the Spanish Civil War.

Many trawler men were so concerned about the significance of the phenomenon that they remained in port that night. A fisherman from the town of Deal in Kent said: "It appeared as if the whole heavens were on fire, and great beams of red light like steps stretched across the sky."

Just six weeks after this spectacular event, Hitler annexed Austria on 12th March 1938 and later that year he annexed the Sudetenland border regions of Czechoslovakia. The land grab by Germany and a new era of war with the most terrible consequences, had effectively begun. This terrible war would claim the lives of 85 million people, including those dying from war related famine and disease.

So the chastisement of war that Our Lady warned us would happen if we did not cease offending God came to pass, because we ignored her requests to turn from sin, to consecrate Russia to Her Immaculate Heart and to take up the Communion of Reparation on the First Five Saturdays.

The legacy after the end of World War II was the beginning of the Cold War, with communist Russia spreading her errors throughout the world, causing wars and persecutions of the Church, just as Mary had warned us about!

Unfortunately sinfulness in the world today is orders of magnitude worse than it was in 1917, especially through atheism and abortion, and so we're now surely exposing ourselves to a far greater chastisement than World War II.

At both Lourdes and Fatima the children were completely immersed in joy, love and exultation in the presence of Our Lady and perhaps it was similar to what Peter, James and John experienced at the Transfiguration.

Our Lady last appeared to Bernadette on 16th July 1858 on the Feast of Our Lady of Mount Carmel, and it's unlikely to be a coincidence that the last time the children of Fatima saw the Blessed Virgin, she was dressed as Our Lady of Carmel.

A key theme of the 24 apparitions at Lourdes and Fatima is clearly the need for **repentance** and how the sins of mankind greatly offend God. Also, that there are consequences of sin at the level of the individual and at the macro level, and that it's essential for us to **pray for sinners** and those who don't believe in God.

At Lourdes on the 21st February, Bernadette said that Our Lady looked very sorrowful as she said, "Pray for sinners."

Three days later on 24th February, she said with great sadness, **"Repentance, Repentance, Repentance"** and it was also at this visit that Our Lady said, "Pray to God for the conversion of sinners."

Then on 27th February, Our Lady said to Bernadette, "Kiss the ground on behalf of sinners" and the following day Bernadette once again kissed the ground for the same reason.

Now at Fatima on three of the visits Our Lady spoke of how offended God is by the sins of mankind and on another, that her Immaculate Heart was outraged by the sins of humanity.

And it was on her first visit on 13th May 1917 that Our Lady asked the children:

"Are you willing to offer yourselves to God and bear all the sufferings He wills to send you, **as an act of reparation for the sins by which He is offended**, and of supplication for the conversion of sinners?"

At the 13th June apparition, Mary said, "He wants to establish in the world **devotion to my Immaculate Heart**. I promise salvation to those who embrace it, and those souls will be loved by God like flowers placed by me to adorn his throne."

It was also during this apparition that Lucia saw a heart encircled by thorns, which she described as follows:

"In front of the palm of Our Lady's right hand was a Heart encircled by thorns which pierced it. We understood that this was the Immaculate Heart of Mary, outraged by the sins of humanity, and seeking reparation."

Again on 13th July 1917 at Fatima, Mary said, "Sacrifice yourself for sinners, and say many times, especially when you make some sacrifice: 'O Jesus, it is for love of You, for the conversion of sinners, and in reparation for sins committed against the Immaculate Heart of Mary.'"

It was also on this day that the children were given the vision which later came to be known as the third secret, and in this vision they saw an angel pointing to the earth with his right hand and saying in a loud voice, "**Penance, Penance, Penance**."

These words clearly mirror what Our Lady said to Bernadette at Lourdes on 24th February 1858.

At the 4th visit at Fatima on 19th August 1917, Lucia said that Our Lady looked very sad as she said:

"Pray, pray very much, and make sacrifices for sinners; for many souls go to hell, because there are none to sacrifice themselves and to pray for them."

Again, at the last apparition on 13th October (the day of the Miracle of the Sun), Lucia noticed that the Virgin Mary looked very sad as she said:

"Do not offend the Lord our God any more, because He is already so much offended."

These were the very last words spoken by Our Lady of all the 24 apparitions at Lourdes and Fatima and she must surely have chosen them for a purpose!

So it's quite clear that the key reasons that the Virgin Mary appeared on earth was to warn us of the dangers of sin, to ask us to repent and stop offending God, and to plead with us to pray for sinners.

Repenting of our own sins and turning to prayer will clearly help us as individuals, but it's simply not enough because the collective sins of humanity are so serious that they are constantly offending God. If mankind continues down this path we will surely expose ourselves to a terrible chastisement.

Mary asked us numerous times at both Lourdes and Fatima to pray for sinners and to pray for their conversion, so we perhaps shouldn't see ourselves as stand alone entities, but rather as being a part of the massive jigsaw puzzle of humanity.

Far more weight was given to the theme of sin and the consequences of it at Fatima, where Mary directly linked this to wars, famine, disease and persecutions of the Church.

For a while the call to repentance and conversion that Mary asked for at Lourdes would have been put into effect by many people, but with the passing of time mankind again slipped away from the laws of God.

A more robust approach was therefore needed at Fatima and this would explain why Mary allowed the children there to see a terrifying vision of hell, so that they could tell the world that this state is a reality and not a myth.

Her hope was surely that this would shake people out of their complacency and that it would encourage them to repent and to turn to God in prayer before it was too late.

Reading the accounts of the 24 apparitions there's another thing that stands out and that's the praying of the **Rosary**. The Virgin Mary and Bernadette prayed the Rosary together at the grotto, and at all six apparitions at Fatima Our Lady asked the children to pray the Rosary every day.

When Lucia and her friends first saw the Angel of Peace on a hill called the Cabeco outside Fatima in 1915, they were just about to pray the Rosary together. Similarly, the second time Lucia witnessed this angel was in the Spring of 1916, just after she, Francisco and Jacinta had finished making this devotion.

When Bernadette first saw the Virgin Mary at the grotto she noticed that she had a Rosary hanging on her right arm and then Bernadette instinctively took her own Rosary out of her pocket and began praying.

At the first of the Fatima Apparitions on 13th May 1917, Lucia bravely asked Our Lady if she would go to heaven, and Our Lady responded that she would indeed go there. She then asked whether Jacinta would go to heaven and was assured that she would also make it into heaven.

But when Lucia asked whether Francisco would go there also, she replied, "He will go there too, but he must say many Rosaries."

It was also on this day that Our Lady said:

"Pray the Rosary every day, in order to obtain peace for the world, and the end of the war."

Later, on 13th July 1917 when Lucia asked Our Lady, "What do you want of me?" she replied:

"I want you to come here on the 13th of next month, to continue to pray the Rosary every day, in honour of Our Lady of the Rosary, in order to obtain peace for the world and the end of the war, because only she can help you."

She also said to the children on that same day, "When you pray the Rosary, say after each mystery: 'O my Jesus, forgive us, save us from the fires of hell. Lead all souls to heaven, especially those who are most in need."

Then at Our Lady's 5th visit to Fatima on 13th September she said, "Continue to pray the Rosary in order to obtain the end of the war."

Finally, at the 6th and last apparition at Fatima, Our Lady announced to Lucia, Francisco and Jacinta: **"I am the Lady of the Rosary."**

So it's plain to see from what Mary said at the 24 apparitions that praying the Rosary has immense spiritual value, that it contributes to peace in the world and that it helps souls on their journey to heaven.

This is also evident because a large part of the First Five Saturdays devotion that Our Lady called for involves the Rosary and reflecting on its mysteries.

Mary is the most effective and powerful intercessor we could ever ask for, and her desire to draw us away from sin, to save souls from hell and to convert atheists is perfectly aligned with the will of Almighty God.

No human being could possibly know Jesus like Mary does, as she held Jesus in her arms after his birth in Bethlehem, and she held him in her arms after he died at Calvary.

The wedding feast at Cana illustrates just how attentive Jesus is to the voice of his mother and so we can have confidence that she will always intercede to him on our behalf.

We can also take great comfort from the beautiful promise that she made to us, that she will be present at our death with the graces necessary for our salvation, if we will just make the First Five Saturdays devotion.

"Look, my daughter, at my Heart, surrounded with thorns with which ungrateful men pierce me at every moment by their blasphemies and ingratitude. You can at least try to console me and say that I promise to assist at the hour of death, with the graces necessary for salvation, all those who, for five consecutive months, shall confess, receive Holy Communion, recite five decades of the Rosary, and keep me company for fifteen minutes while meditating on the fifteen mysteries of the Rosary, with the intention of making reparation to me."

- Chapter 9 -

The Rosary

The Rosary played an important part in all 24 apparitions at Lourdes and Fatima, and Our Lady linked the making of this devotion with peace in our world and with the conversion of sinners. Mary also declared at Fatima: **"I am the Lady of the Rosary."**

It's significant also that Bernadette and Francisco both died and were buried with a Rosary in their hands!

The Our Father prayer at the start of each decade of the Rosary was given to us by Jesus himself, and the Hail Mary comes in part from the greeting of the Angel Gabriel at the Annunciation and also Elizabeth's greeting to Mary when she visited her in Judea (the Visitation).

As we pray each of the five decades we're meant to contemplate one of the mysteries of the Rosary. The same is true when we make the First Five Saturdays devotion, which Mary revealed to Lucia on 10th December 1925. This involves going to confession, receiving communion, reciting the Rosary, and spending another fifteen minutes meditating on the fifteen mysteries, on five consecutive first Saturdays of the month.

She said that these four elements had to be made with the intention of making reparation for the sins against Her Immaculate Heart, and the reason that the devotion is made over five Saturdays is that there are five main sins involved.

The first is to deny the Immaculate Conception and the second is to deny Mary's Perpetual Virginity. The third sin is to deny Her Divine Maternity, in other words that she gave birth to the Son of God, and also a refusal to recognise her as the Mother of all Men.

The other sin is to make children become indifferent or scornful towards Mary because of the things that we say to them, and the last sins involve blasphemies against Mary in holy images of her.

There follows a description of all 20 mysteries of the Rosary, including the Mysteries of Light (Luminous mysteries), which John Paul II announced in 2002 and which cover some of the key events in the three year public ministry of Jesus.

The Annunciation

The angel Gabriel appeared to Mary saying, "Greetings you who are highly favoured! The Lord is with you." Gabriel then announced that Mary would conceive through the Holy Spirit and carry the Son of God in her womb and he also revealed that Elizabeth, her relative, was herself six months pregnant.

Mary's calm acceptance of this unique role and her deep faith in God are an example for all of us as Christians.

She simply responded, "I am the Lord's servant. May it be to me as you have said."

The Visitation

Mary made the journey from Nazareth to a small town in Judea to stay with her relative Elizabeth for three months. If the town where Elizabeth lived was Ein Karem, as some historians believe, then it would have been very arduous for Mary as this is 145 kilometres from Nazareth.

The child in Elizabeth's womb jumped for joy at hearing Mary's voice and Elizabeth said:

"Blessed are you among women, and blessed is the child you will bear!"

Our Lady then sang a song in praise of God, which we know today as The Magnificat.

Mary lived here until shortly before Elizabeth gave birth to John the Baptist, the last of the prophets of the Old Testament.

The Nativity

Joseph and Mary travelled all the way from Nazareth to Bethlehem, which is a distance of about 156 kilometres, under very difficult circumstances as Mary was heavily pregnant at the time. This was to comply with the decree of Caesar Augustus that everyone had to travel to his home town in order to register for a population census.

After Mary gave birth, three devotees of the religion of Zoroastrianism visited the Holy Family, having travelled all the way from Persia to worship the new born Messiah.

They brought gold to signify the divinity and kingship of Jesus, as well as frankincense, the fragrant white resin which was burned as an offering to God and which signified the holiness of the child Jesus.

They also presented him with myrrh, a spice derived from the resin of the low growing myrrh tree, which was used in the embalming process.

This gift was symbolic of suffering and was prophetic, as Jesus was offered the anaesthetising myrrh mixed with wine at his crucifixion, but he refused to drink it. Joseph of Arimathea and Nicodemus would later use myrrh and aloes to embalm the body of Jesus.

The Presentation

On the eighth day, Joseph and Mary took Jesus to the temple to be circumcised as required by Mosaic Law, and they were met by a devout Jew named Simeon in the Temple Courts.

It had been revealed to Simeon by the Holy Spirit that he wouldn't die until he'd seen the Christ of God. Simeon praised and blessed Mary and Joseph, but he also cautioned Mary that a sword would pierce her soul, and this was one of the seven dolours or sorrows that she would have in her life.

Finding in the Temple

Mary, Joseph and the 12 year old Jesus went up to Jerusalem for the annual celebration of the Passover, but unknown to his parents Jesus didn't join the caravan going back to Nazareth. They anxiously searched for him but only found Jesus three days later in the temple at Jerusalem, sitting with all the teachers of The Law.

Luke 2:48: When his parents saw him, they were astonished. His mother said to him, "Son, why have you treated us like this? Your father and I have been anxiously searching for you."

"Why were you searching for me?" he asked. "Didn't you know I had to be in my Father's house?"

The agony in the garden

After the last supper, Jesus crossed the Kidron valley with his disciples and walked to an olive grove called Gethsemane to pray. After a while he went a little deeper into the garden with his most trusted companions, Peter, James and John and it was here that he made the great act of faith that we can all imitate in times of difficulty or suffering:

'Father, if you are willing, take this cup from me; yet not my will, but yours be done.'

Jesus knew the terrible pain that he was about to endure, and in this anxious state his sweat looked like blood as it fell to the ground according to Luke, who was himself a physician.

This is a rare medical condition which happens under conditions of great stress, when the capillaries around the sweat glands constrict and later dilate to the extent that blood enters the sweat glands.

Judas Iscariot then arrived with the chief priests and a large cohort of the Temple Guard, and he then walked over to kiss Jesus on the cheek, prompting Jesus to ask, "Judas, are you betraying the Son of Man with a kiss?"

It was then that Peter drew his sword and struck out at Malchus, the servant of the High Priest, cutting off his right ear. But Jesus, forever filled with compassion, performed his last miracle while alive on earth by healing him.

He was then taken to the house of Caiaphas, where the Temple guards blindfolded Jesus, hit him and said, "Prophesy to us, Christ! Who hit you?"

He was questioned by the Sanhedrin and it was here that the High Priest asked him, "Are you the Christ, the Son of the Blessed One?"

Jesus replied, "I am. And you will see the Son of Man sitting at the right hand of the Mighty One and coming on the clouds of heaven."

It was also here that Peter denied knowing Jesus three times, just as Jesus had foretold at the Last Supper.

The scourging at the pillar

Jesus was taken to Pontius Pilate in the Praetorium to be questioned, but the Roman Governor could find no fault in him at all, despite all the charges brought against him by the Chief Priests and Elders.

As Pilate was sitting on the judge's seat, his wife Claudia Procula sent him an urgent message saying, "Don't have anything to do with that innocent man, for I have suffered a great deal today in a dream because of him."

Pilate offered to have Jesus released, but the crowd was whipped up by the Chief Priests to ask for a criminal named Barabbas to be set free instead. Barabbas was a murderer who'd previously taken part in a riot in Jerusalem.

Pilate then washed his hands in front of the Jews, saying, "I am innocent of this man's blood," before having Jesus taken away to be flogged and crucified.

Now unlike the Jewish flogging of 40 lashes which traditionally ended at 39, the Roman scourging was very brutal and had no limit on the number of strikes. In fact it was called a 'half death' because it was designed to bring the victims close to death so that they would spend less time hanging on their crosses.

The crowning with thorns

Then the entire company of soldiers in the Praetorium surrounded Jesus and began to mock and beat him. They stripped Jesus, dressed him in a scarlet robe and then twisted some thorns into a crown and put it on his head.

Then they put a staff in his right hand and mocked him by kneeling on the ground and saying, "Hail, king of the Jews!"

The soldiers beat Jesus on the head over and over again with a staff and spat on him, and after the beating they took the scarlet robe off Jesus and put his own clothes back on him. Jesus was then led away to be given his cross and to begin the agonising walk along the Via Dolorosa to Calvary.

Carrying of the cross

Jesus was then led from the Praetorium carrying either the full cross or the beam of the cross, called the Patibulum. The full cross is estimated to have weighed 135 kilograms and the beam would have weighed up to 60 kilograms.

By now Jesus was so weakened from the beatings and the scourging that he stumbled and fell for the first time, and tradition tells us that it was then that he met his beloved mother.

The soldiers then forced a man named Simon from Cyrene to carry the cross or to help carry it for the rest of the walk to Calvary. Simon is believed to have been a member of the large Jewish community who lived in Cyrene in Libya and was probably visiting Jerusalem for the Passover celebrations, with his two sons Alexander and Rufus.

It was then that a woman, traditionally called Veronica, ignoring the hostile crowd and the soldiers, rushed up to Jesus and handed him a sweat towel or Sudarium with which to wipe the blood and sweat from his face.

For showing such compassion, she was rewarded with an imprint of the face of Jesus on the towel. The real name of this brave woman is uncertain, as Veronica is a fusion of the Latin words 'Vera' for true and 'Icon' for image.

Jesus fell for a second time, and it was then that he saw several of the women who'd helped him on his three year ministry. He turned and said to them, "Daughters of Jerusalem, do not weep for me; weep for yourselves and for your children." Jesus then fell for a third time before finally reaching Golgotha.

The crucifixion

Jesus was offered wine mixed with myrrh, but he refused to drink it, and he was then nailed to the cross by four guards between two thieves named Dismas and Gestas.

Jesus forgave the soldiers who were crucifying him, saying, "**Father, forgive them, for they do not know what they are doing.**" This was the first of seven statements that Jesus made from the cross.

Pilate had a notice pinned to the cross which read 'King of the Jews,' much to the anger of the chief priests and elders standing there. The soldiers then cast lots for the undergarment of Jesus, as was prophesied by David in Psalm 22, which was written a thousand years earlier.

Gestas mocked Jesus along with the crowds walking past the cross, but he was rebuked by Dismas who then turned to Jesus and said, "Jesus remember me when you come into your kingdom."

Jesus replied, "**I tell you the truth, today you will be with me in paradise.**"

At about midday, the sky became dark, and this darkness persisted for a period of three hours. In his work, 'History of the Olympiads,' the historian Phlegon wrote that it was so dark that the stars were plainly visible, and the phenomenon was also described by Tertullian in 'The Apologeticum.'

This darkness is inexplicable to scientists because it couldn't have been caused by a total solar eclipse, as these can only happen at the time of a new moon, and Passover is always celebrated at the time of a full moon! Also, the longest time that a solar eclipse can possibly last is 7 minutes and 31 seconds.

Jesus saw his mother standing nearby with Mary Magdalene and Mary the wife of Clopas, and he said to his mother, "**Dear woman, here is your son.**"

He then said to the disciple John, "**Here is your mother.**"

Mark wrote that it was at the ninth hour (3 pm) that Jesus uttered the words, "**Eloi, Eloi, Lama Sabachthani?**" meaning "**My God, My God, why have you forsaken me?**"

When Jesus was alive on earth, he was at all times fully divine and fully human, and this cry of anguish and despair was made by Jesus the man, who was by now at the point of death. However, the words Jesus spoke are also the beginning of the wonderful Psalm 22 written by King David, which actually prophesied the crucifixion and the second part of this Psalm is all about praise of God.

Jesus then said, "**I am thirsty,**" which prompted one of the bystanders to dip a sponge in vinegar, which he then held up on a hyssop stick for Jesus to drink.

After this, Jesus then said, "**It is accomplished**."

Luke's Gospel is unique in that it records the last words of Jesus being, "**Father, into your hands I commit my spirit**."

Jesus died after having hung for six hours on the cross at Calvary, and immediately there was a major earthquake, which was also described by the historian Phlegon and for which there is also geological evidence.

At the very moment of Christ's death, the great curtain in the Temple of Jerusalem, which was over 60 feet high and four inches thick, was torn in half, thus exposing the 'Holy of Holies.'

This section of the temple was reserved for the High Priest and he would walk through the curtain into the Holy of Holies to offer sacrifice for man's sins. God's plan of establishing a new and everlasting covenant with man had been accomplished, and now that Jesus had died for the transgressions of Mankind, he himself had become the sacrifice for our sins.

When the crowds who'd been mocking Jesus saw all these miraculous events, they walked away from Calvary beating their chests. Even the pagan centurion Longinus who was standing guard at the cross said, "Surely this man was the Son of God!"

The two thieves were ultimately killed by having their legs broken by the soldiers, which meant that they could no longer push themselves up against the foot block on their crosses in order to catch a breath.

However, as Jesus was already dead, Longinus thrust a lance into his side and immediately blood and water gushed forth from the wound. Tradition has it that Longinus, who'd suffered from poor eyesight, was sprayed in the face when he did this, and he was miraculously healed. So even in death, Jesus brought about miraculous healings! This tradition also holds that Longinus converted to Christianity after having witnessed the incredible events at Calvary that day.

Jesus was taken down from the cross by Nicodemus and Joseph of Arimathea, and they used 34 kilograms of myrrh and aloes with strips of linen to embalm his body. Once they'd finished, the two men moved a large rock across the entrance of the tomb and this was later sealed by the Roman guard that was positioned there at the request of the Chief Priests. This Roman 'guard' would have comprised at least four soldiers.

The resurrection

There was another earthquake in Jerusalem on the Sunday morning, and this was presumably an aftershock after the severe earthquake of the previous Friday afternoon.

The Gospels tell us that an angel appeared and rolled back the massive stone which had been placed across the entrance to the tomb. The terrified guards then ran off to report what they'd just witnessed to the chief priests, because they were too scared to tell Pilate that the body that they'd been guarding was now missing.

The tomb was found empty early that morning by Mary Magdalene, Mary the mother of James, Joanna and some other women (according to Luke's gospel).

Mary Magdalene was the first person to see and to talk to the resurrected Jesus, and she was the first to give witness of the resurrection to the apostles who were in hiding at the time. It was for this reason that Saint Augustine of Hippo gave her the title, 'Apostle to the Apostles.'

On hearing Mary Magdalene's account, Peter and John then ran over to the burial site near Calvary and entered the tomb, where they both saw the discarded strips of linen that had covered the head and body of Jesus.

Jesus later appeared to the disciples in the upper room and he ate in front of them to put them at ease, but Thomas wasn't present that day and he refused to believe that Jesus had in fact risen from the dead.

One week later Jesus appeared again and this time Thomas was present. Jesus asked him to put his finger in the holes in his hands and to put his hand into his side where the lance had entered and he said, "Stop doubting and believe."

The stunned Thomas could only utter that great declaration of faith, "My Lord and my God!"

Jesus then said, "Because you have seen me, you have believed; blessed are those who have not seen and yet have believed."

The Ascension

Jesus appeared to his disciples for forty days, during which time he continued to teach them and he also ate with them on several occasions, which shows that a resurrected body is not just spirit.

Jesus was then taken up into Heaven in front of his disciples outside the town of Bethany which is just a few kilometres from Jerusalem, and it was in this town that his friends Martha, Mary and Lazarus lived.

The raising of Lazarus from the dead after he'd been buried for four days was arguably the most spectacular miracle that Jesus worked, and it was this miracle that had made the Chief Priests determined to have Jesus put to death.

As the apostles were staring up into the sky, two angels appeared and gave an assurance to them that Jesus would one day return to the earth in the same way that he had left.

Descent of the Holy Spirit

Before his passion, Jesus had asked the disciples to remain in Jerusalem until they'd received the gift of the Holy Spirit, and so they waited in the upper room of their house behind a locked door, because they feared being arrested by the Jews.

Ten days after the Ascension, the disciples were baptised by the Holy Spirit, who appeared as tongues of fire above their heads, and this was the baptism of fire that John the Baptist had spoken of by the River Jordan.

A very powerful wind blew around the house as this was happening, and this quickly drew the attention of a large crowd of people who converged on the building.

Peter then emerged and gave a speech which all in the crowd understood, despite the fact that they were from many different countries and spoke a variety of languages.

He urged them all to repent and to be baptised in the name of Jesus, and three thousand did so that day alone.

The Assumption

Christian tradition has always held that Mary was assumed into Heaven, both body and soul, immediately after she had died. For example the Feast of the Assumption was celebrated in Syria from as far back as the 5th century and it was celebrated in Jerusalem from the 6th century onwards.

Pope Pius XII exercised papal infallibility on this teaching on the 1st of November 1950 and the 15th of August was set aside as the Feast of the Assumption.

The Virgin Mary was conceived without sin and lived her life without sin and so she was able to be taken directly into Heaven.

The Coronation

It was also Pope Pius XII who established the 22nd of August as the feast date of the Coronation in the Church in 1954, but the origin of the tradition can be found in **Revelation 12:1**:

'A great and wondrous sign appeared in heaven: a woman clothed with the sun, with the moon under her feet and a crown of twelve stars on her head.'

The chapter goes on to describe the fall of Satan and his angels and the fight against the woman and her offspring.

Revelation 12:17: 'Then the dragon was enraged at the woman and went off to make war against the rest of her offspring – those who obey God's commandments and hold to the testimony of Jesus.'

This theme mirrors the account in Genesis after the Fall of Man, where there was enmity between the Serpent and the woman and her offspring.

Mary was uniquely chosen from the beginning by God to bring the Christ into our World and her special role continues as our spiritual mother in Heaven.

She constantly intercedes on our behalf to Jesus and tries to draw all people away from sin and to his love. Her mission of the salvation of souls is therefore diametrically opposed to that of Satan.

Baptism of Jesus

Jesus was baptised at the age of thirty by John the Baptist in the River Jordan and it was John that had called the Jews to a baptism of repentance for the forgiveness of sins. As soon as Jesus came up out of the water, John saw heaven being 'torn open' and the Holy Spirit descended on Jesus in the form of a dove.

The voice of God was heard saying, "You are my Son, whom I love; with you I am well pleased."

It was immediately after his baptism that Jesus went into the wilderness to fast and pray for forty days to prepare himself for his public ministry and for his later passion.

Jesus clearly had no need to be baptised at all, but he set us all an example to follow by doing this, and it's through the sacrament of baptism that we are born into the death and resurrection of Jesus and so become a party to the new covenant.

Wedding at Cana:

This wedding marked the beginning of the three year public ministry of Jesus, and he was there with his mother Mary, but not his father, and it's thought that Joseph had died by then. When the hosts ran out of wine, Mary brought this to the attention of her son, and initially Jesus seemed reluctant to get involved because he said, "Dear woman, why do you involve me? My time has not yet come."

But undeterred, Mary told the attendants to do whatever Jesus asked, having full confidence that he would work a miracle. There were six stone jars nearby, holding in total between 450 and 690 litres of water and Jesus converted this into the very best of wines, so it could be argued that this miracle is an example of transubstantiation. It also shows how Jesus listens to the voice of his mother and this surely gives us confidence in her power as an intercessor for us! It's also interesting that the Eastern Orthodox Church holds that the bridegroom at this wedding was Simon the Zealot, who would become one of the apostles.

Proclamation of God's kingdom

The public ministry of Jesus with his apostles lasted for three years and he appointed 72 men to go out throughout the towns and villages ahead of him to prepare the way.

He worked an astonishing array of miracles including the feeding of the five thousand and the four thousand with just a few loaves of bread and a few fish. These numbers were just men, so the figure including women and children would have been considerably higher than this!

He also raised at least three people from the dead, including the son of a poor widow from the town of Nain and the twelve year old daughter of Jairus, a synagogue ruler.

But he worked arguably his greatest miracle, when he raised Lazarus to life in the town of Bethany after he'd been dead for four days. The raising of Lazarus was the final straw for the chief priests and elders who convened a meeting of the 69 strong Great Sanhedrin at which they agreed to have Jesus arrested and put to death.

John 11:27: Then the chief priests and the Pharisees called a meeting of the Sanhedrin. "What are we accomplishing?" they asked.

"Here is this man performing many miraculous signs. If we let him go on like this, everyone will believe in him, and then the Romans will come and take away both our place and our nation."

The miracles worked by Jesus were also described by reliable historians from antiquity such as Josephus and Tertullian.

Josephus wrote in his work 'Testimonium flavianum' in 93 AD:

'About this time there lived Jesus, a wise man, if indeed one ought to call him a man. For he was one who performed surprising deeds and was a teacher of such people as accept the truth gladly. He won over many Jews and many of the Greeks.'

The yoke of Jesus was light compared to the rigour of Mosaic Law and his teachings centered around true spirituality, mercy and love for fellow man, as in the Parable of the Good Samaritan.

The Transfiguration

Jesus took Peter, James and John up a high mountain, where he was transfigured before their eyes. Mark wrote that his clothes became dazzlingly white and Matthew records that his face 'shone like the sun.' Moses and Elijah then appeared and spoke with Jesus and the voice of God was heard to say: "This is my Son, whom I love. Listen to him!"

This was one of three occasions described in the gospels where the voice of God was clearly audible, and if the apostles had any doubt whatsoever that Jesus was indeed the Son of God, they would have disappeared at that very instant.

The transfiguration showed the three apostles the glorious state of a resurrected body, which all people who die in God's love will have.

Institution of Holy Eucharist

During his ministry Jesus had often referred to himself as being 'the Bread of Life.'

John 6:47: "I tell you the truth, he who believes has everlasting life. I am the bread of life. Your forefathers ate the manna in the desert, yet they died. But there is the bread that comes down from heaven, which a man may eat and not die. I am the living bread that comes down from heaven. If anyone eats of this bread, he will live forever. This bread is my flesh, which I will give for the life of the world."

Then the Jews began to argue sharply among themselves, "How can this man give us his flesh to eat?"

Jesus said to them, "I tell you the truth, unless you eat the flesh of the Son of Man and drink his blood, you have no life in you. Whoever eats my flesh and drinks my blood has eternal life, and I will raise him up at the last day.

"For my flesh is real food and my blood is real drink. Whoever eats my flesh and drinks my blood remains in me, and I in him. Just as the living Father sent me and I live because of the Father, so the one who feeds on me will live because of me. This is the bread that came down from heaven. Your forefathers ate manna

and died, but he who feeds on this bread will live forever." He said this while teaching in the synagogue in Capernaum.

Jesus waited until the last night before his arrest and passion to share this meal with his disciples, as by doing this it would have the maximum effect and his words would be emblazoned in their minds forever.

Luke 22:19: And he took bread, gave thanks and broke it, and gave it to them, saying, "This is my body given for you; do this in remembrance of me."

Matthew 26:27: Then he took a cup, and when he had given thanks, he gave it to them, saying, "Drink from it, all of you. This is my blood of the covenant, which is poured out for many for the forgiveness of sins. I tell you, I will not drink from this fruit of the vine from now on until that day when I drink it anew with you in my Father's kingdom."

Jesus gave himself up as a sacrifice for our sins and so put right the relationship between God and His creation which had been fractured through disobedience. All who are baptised, and who believe that Jesus is the Son of God are a party to the new covenant that he established, which rewards us with the unimaginable gift of eternal life.

1 Corinthians 2:9: No eye has seen, no ear has heard, no mind has conceived what God has prepared for those who love Him.